HEALING YOU, HEALING ME
A DIVORCE SUPPORT GROUP LEADER'S GUIDE

CHAMPION PRESS, LTD.
FREDONIA, WISCONSIN
Copyright © 2004 Micki McWade

All rights reserved. No part of this book shall be reproduced, stored, or transmitted by any means without written permission from the publisher. Although every precaution has been taken in the preparation of this book, the publisher and author assume no responsibility for errors or omissions. Neither is any liability assumed for damages resulting from the use of the information contained herein. For more information contact: Champion Press, Ltd. 4308 Blueberry Road, Fredonia, Wisconsin 53021 www.championpress.com

Reasonable care has been taken in the preparation of the text to insure its clarity and accuracy. The book is sold with the understanding that the author and publisher are not engaged in rendering professional service. The author and publisher specifically disclaim any liability, loss or risk, personal or otherwise, which is incurred as a consequence, directly or indirectly, of the use and application of any of the contents of this book.

ISBN 1-891400-65-7
LCCN: 2004105937

MANUFACTURED IN THE UNITED STATES OF AMERICA

10 9 8 7 6 5 4 3 2 1

This book is dedicated to support group leaders who give their time, creativity and compassion to make life better and inspire others to heal and go on, despite difficult circumstances of all kinds.

Acknowledgements

I would like to acknowledge and thank Elizabeth Sullivan, who has been with me as co-leader of our original group since the beginning in 1993. Laurie S. and Mary P. took on the leadership of the next group formed in White Plains, NY and have done a wonderful job. I truly appreciate their service. Sally F. has graciously and competently taken over for Elizabeth and me and now is dedicated to continuing the work in Mt. Kisco, NY. I am grateful to have our group in such good hands. All have all served as trusted advisors when I had issues to resolve.

There have been many people who have lead the break-out groups over the years and our meetings would not have been as good without them: Bette, Susan, Neil, Ruth—thank you all.

I would like to thank my husband, Gary Ditlow, and my children, Meredith and her husband, Andrew Sevin, Charlie, Megan and Joe McWade for their continued patience with my being unavailable while I have lead meetings and continued to write over the years. They have all been supportive in different ways and I am very grateful for all of it.

I would like to thank my grandson, Harrison James Sevin, for being adorable and a wonderful distraction when I needed a break.

I wish to express appreciation to my editor and publisher, Brook Noel, for her faith in my work and willingness to publish my books. Her expertise has made a great difference on all three of my books so far.

I am grateful for my friend, Dr. Pamela D. Blair's mentoring and inspiration to work in this field and for Al Frankel's and Mel Schwartz' guidance at other critical times.

St. Mark's Episcopal Church, Mt. Kisco has been our group's home for 11 years at this writing and we are deeply grateful for the hospitality and generosity the Rector, Stephen Voysey has bestowed on our group.

I have had the honor and privilege to witness and share in the lives of hundreds of people who have participated in the groups. I want to acknowledge the courage it takes to walk in the door and be with us. Thank you all for the great gift of trust you have given me. It has truly transformed my life.

Contents

Acknowledgements   5

Section One
Understanding the Importance of Support

Introduction   13

Chapter One
On Divorce Support   19

Chapter Two
On Leadership: Understanding What Is Our
Responsibility, and What Isn't   32

Chapter Three
An Overview of Divorce Recovery   44

Section Two
Building A Support Group

Chapter Four
Getting a Divorce Group Started   54

Chapter Five
Creating a Safe Place   64

Chapter Six
Leading a Meeting   70

Chapter Seven
 Dealing with Difficult People   88

Chapter Eight
Dating within the Group   96

SECTION THREE
Meeting Tool Box

Chapter Nine
 Meeting Topics   104

Chapter Ten
Twelve Step Separation/Divorce Recovery
Group Meeting format   128

Chapter Eleven
Leader's Essays   140

Chapter Twelve
A Leader's Checklist   164

Chapter Thirteen
Sample Meeting Brochure   168

Bibliography 174

SECTION I

UNDERSTANDING THE IMPORTANCE OF SUPPORT

Introduction

As I sat in the circle that first night, questions raced through my mind. Who was I to be leading a meeting? Was this just a crazy idea? I quickly scanned the other faces, all looking at me expectantly. I certainly didn't know all the answers, and had a number of questions myself. Would this work? Once here, would they come back? What would keep people coming?

I had been helped in a group setting before and wanted to work with others again. In the fall of 1993, I had been separated from my husband of 23 years for about two years, had four children, lots of worries plus some ideas about recovery. Creating a group would help me sort it all out because I wouldn't be struggling alone for a change. I knew of others who had some answers of their own and I wanted to hear about them. If we shared our experience, strength and hope maybe we could help each other survive this unbelievably hard time.

I opened the meeting as if I knew what I was doing, but expected to be challenged by those who came: What are your qualifications? Are you a therapist? What training have you had? That didn't happen. (Although I am a clinical social worker now, I was not a professional at the time.)

Everyone was so grateful to find a place to talk about divorce and separation issues that they thanked me profusely instead. I heard "Micki, what a great idea! This is wonderful! I'll definitely be back next week. Thanks for setting this up. It's so helpful to be able to talk about all this with people who get it." "My family is tired of hearing about this so I'm glad to have a place to talk." "My children are happy to see that I'm getting some help. They've been worried about me."

That was almost eleven years ago. Hundreds of people have come and gone and the meeting goes on today. I passed the baton after nine years to a person who has been in the group almost as long as I have and it's still is going strong. I stop in once a month now.

Another satisfying experience has been the reunions that take place every year on the anniversary of our first meeting when we invite former members to come back and share what they have learned so far with new people who are sure they are not going to live through their divorce. I know today, from a long-term perspective, what an impact belonging to our group has had. I have heard their gratitude expressed over and over—what a great reward!

"This group was a lifeline to me when I felt no one else understood." "The group helped me understand how important it is not to lean on my children for support and gave me the appropriate support I needed." "At a time when I believed no one cared about me, I connected with a wonderful group of people who did care about me and I cared about all of them." "I don't know what I would have done without my group! Before I joined I spent all my time by myself. Now I have friends and we go out to a movie or to dinner on the weekends. I can't tell you how much this has helped me." "At a time when I had no one from my former life to talk to, I used the phone list from the meeting and I didn't feel so alone."

Will you hear these kinds of comments? Yes, you will. Will you be transformed by the experience? Absolutely. For more than my word on the subject, read Chapter Eleven written by group leaders and you'll see for yourself.

You'll come to understand that leading a meeting and being an example of strength and hope is rather heroic. People will be grateful for your commitment and dedication. For those of us who have done it, it has been one of the most satisfying activities of our lives and it may be for you too.

Healing You, Healing Me will provide you with the step-by-step information you need to set up, facilitate and keep a group going. In addition, I have created ongoing support for leaders through email and phone. You can learn more about this support by calling me at 845-424-4522 or sending an email to Micki@12stepdivorce.org. You will not have to do this alone.

As always, when we provide thoughtful service to others, we benefit ourselves. By creating support for others, I created it for myself. You've heard the expression, "What goes around comes around," right? This is a chance to create positive flow in your direction.

We also develop new skills, become more compassionate, increase tolerance and understanding and become better listeners. These attributes will certainly help us in our present and future relationships. Those of us who lead meetings have experienced blessings of all kinds—particularly deeper healing from divorce and greater understanding of ourselves and others.

Who couldn't use the benefits group leadership can bring? With all that said, I hope you will continue the journey through this book and begin your own supportive community..

As this book is going to press, I am working on setting up a group leaders' training and supervision so no leader or potential leader will be left without guidance. You are welcome to call 845-424-4522 for further information.

A telephone meeting is in operation on a telephone bridge line and you are welcome to call in and get an idea of how a meeting of this type is presented. Again, call 845-424-4522 for further information or check the website: www.12stepdivorce.org for details.

WEEKLY TELECONFERENCE MEETING
TWELVE STEP
DIVORCE GROUP

Call in to a telephone bridge—
from home or anywhere.

Call 845-424-4522 to get the
bridge line phone number.

Hear from others who share their
experience, strength and hope!

A place to share and learn.

Tuesday nights at 9 PM,
Eastern time

CHAPTER ONE
ON DIVORCE SUPPORT

I used the word "divorce" in this book as a general term, also referring to the breakup of a couple who wasn't married. The suggestions in this book will work in most situations where there has been a breakup of a significant relationship. As we know, when a relationship is over, there is a great deal of pain involved, regardless of a legal agreement. Marriage, however, also implies that there will be legal ramifications in addition to the emotional ones, which create another level of stress.

As people move through a separation or divorce, the collection of experiences we face can be devastating. The degree of devastation is influenced by the personality of the individual and the support available from others. Research has shown time and time again that we survive difficulty of all kinds if we feel supported by family and friends. If we surround ourselves with those who care for us, we do better—much better— than those who go it alone.

A divorce support group creates an understanding and supportive community of peers who have patience for the process and empathy for what it takes to survive it, long after our family and friends have had enough. By facilitating a group, we create another form of that community for ourselves and others.

Without community, people experience isolation. Isolation presents a significant difficulty while going through divorce and is brought on by a number of factors. Often we find ourselves cut off from people who were in our lives regularly, like our partner's family and friends. We may also be disconnected from friends whom we knew as a couple.

Many people feel profound shame at the failure of a relationship or marriage. We may isolate ourselves because of feelings of remorse and regret about what could have been done differently. A degree of depression is usually present, which furthers our negative feelings. Children are upset, angry and needy, demanding of our attention which makes it hard to find time for ourselves. Some of us are separated from our children and we miss our daily contact with them.

Creating a community where those facing and divorce feel welcomed, encouraged, and learn coping strategies is invaluable and can't be overstated. Yet a group is only as successful as we make it. Successful groups depend on healthy ideas, policies and practices. That is the subject of this book—learning the "tools of the trade" to run an effective and supportive group.

The group purpose is to teach and inspire hope. When one person in a couple learns new tools and experiences an attitude shift, over time that better attitude will change the way the couple relates to each other, which in turn has a positive influence on the couple's children.

So, not only will you be helping group members cope and feel better, you will be helping their children indirectly. If parents are okay, the kids do well. When adults know there's a place to find understanding and support, they will feel encouraged. When stress is reduced more attention can be given to the children who experience their own grief about their parents' divorce.

Facilitating a group may also save a life. When divorcing people are isolated, depressed and without support, it can feel like there is no purpose for living. Some group members report that their week-to-week survival was inspired by the thought of getting to the next group meeting, where they would feel welcome, included and understood. Some reported that they actually counted the days between meetings until they could be with people like themselves. I have also heard people say that they held onto the meeting brochure and read it many times between meetings. It helped them feel connected.

Men often face a bigger challenge in staying connected to supportive people. Many men rely on their partners for social connection so when they lose their significant other, they may lose that connection. Women, on the other hand, are more natural emotional networkers and usually have, or quickly make supportive friends. Men appreciate the opportunity to belong to a group where they can be themselves and not have to put on brave faces and pretend everything is fine.

After awhile, if members keep coming, bonds are formed and they rely on each other for support, feedback and ideas. On the other hand, some will only come to one or two meetings and there are a number of reasons for that. Those who are not ready to accept their divorce can't talk about it or hear others talk about theirs. Some have unrealistic expectations of the group and expect to feel healed immediately, which obviously isn't going to happen. Some will expect a singles group and be disappointed to find that the group is a working group where self-exploration is expected.

> **Tip:** We advise new people, often on the initial phone inquiry, that they should not decide whether or not the group is for them after one meeting. It takes four or five meetings to get to know people and begin to feel comfortable.

Those who have gone through a divorce realize the trauma and crisis of the experience. There is recovery work to be done on many levels: getting over the shock, coping with feelings of rejection and guilt, helping children deal with the loss of a parent in their home, having to fend for oneself, getting through financial crises, recreating our lives in a new context and many more. It takes a long time to work through the aftermath of divorce.

From a medical perspective, Mark Banschick, a child and adolescent psychiatrist in New York, sees divorce as a public health issue. The stress factor alone creates the potential for serious health problems. The risk of heart disease and cancer increases significantly during and for awhile after divorce. Automobile accidents increase by a factor of three because of stress and distraction.

Depression and anxiety are understandable reactions to the major changes that take place. These factors affect the quality of our parenting, our job performance, our ability to function in relationships with friends and family, our ability to make sound decisions and manage our finances.

Belonging to a group and having a place to discuss these issues and worries as well as feeling connected with others in a similar situation, is enormously helpful. We realize we are not alone in this experience and just that alone often brings a tremendous feeling of relief.

Within a group, when we listen to those who have had similar problems, made it through the crisis and actually improved the quality of their lives, we are encouraged to hold on through difficult times. A well-run support group offers hope and can be very therapeutic. Likewise, a negative group can be a disaster and send people home feeling more depressed than when they came in. We'll talk about avoiding that outcome in Chapter Seven.

WHERE MOST OF US TURN FOR HELP

The most common way people try to solve divorce-related problems is through lawyers and the legal system. This is not 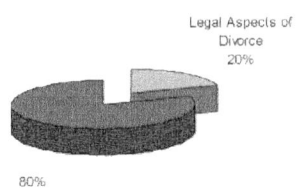 only very expensive, but also painfully inadequate for working through highly emotional issues. Marriage is a legal contract and must be dissolved legally, but the legal piece is only a fraction of what needs to be managed by divorcing people and most attorneys are not trained to handle global family readjustment. Attorneys may inadvertently make the situation worse by the adversarial approach they have been trained to take. We need more help than they can give.

Attorneys are trained in law school to interpret and apply the law to the case at hand. They are not trained in family dynamics. The adversarial approach works well in business situations but when a married couple, and particularly those who are parents of children are pitted against each other, it shreds families. The truth is that when a couple has children they will be connected forever.

FOR THE CHILDREN

Regardless of the separation, who eventually marries who, and where people live, parents remain parents and interaction will be necessary for many years.

> *A critical factor contributing to children's mental health after a divorce is the post-divorce relationship of their parents.*

Children can withstand temporary chaos and discord, but when it goes on over years, damage is done. When access to a much loved parent is greatly curtailed, children suffer. Many books have been written on this topic, but suffice to say for our purposes here, that the way adults handle their divorce greatly impacts their children, both in the long- and short-term.

Forty percent of children in the United States will experience the divorce of their parents. While the support groups discussed here are not for children, supporting their parents' stability has an important impact on their lives.

A support group provides a place where people feel understood and connected. A healthy group also offers a program with suggestions, things to think about, relevant topics and perhaps guest speakers who will further education and inform members. We can't know too much while going through divorce and awareness is greatly expanded by belonging to a group.

FRIENDS AND FAMILY

Sharing with our friends and family helps but that may not be enough. Our circle may grow tired of listening to us talk about this major transition. Those who have not experienced divorce, may find it hard to understand why we need so much time, discussion and assistance to work through it. In contrast, a divorce support group provides an appropriate place to explore our experience from many different angles. We don't have to reinvent the wheel. Why not utilize the experience of others who have gone before us? Some will teach us what works and others will teach us what doesn't. We will learn from either vantage point. A favorite quote comes to mind:

> *If you can't be a good example, then you'll just have to serve as a horrible warning.*
> —Catherine Aird

CRITICAL CHOICE

There are two directions we can go in divorce: we can choose to struggle alone, attempting to keep things the same as they were, or we can be part of a group, learn new skills, and eventually embrace change.

Most groups contain members at various stages of divorce: those who are recently separated, those in the legal process, and those who have been through it all and need time to integrate the experience and adjust. The more experienced people will show newcomers that survival is possible and the newer people will remind others of where they came from and appreciate the progress they've made.

CREATING A NEW SOCIAL CIRCLE

Those of us who have been married a long time may not have single friends. We may be the first in our circle to experience divorce and have no one to guide us. We may suddenly and uncomfortably feel like a fifth wheel in our familiar social setting. To avoid this feeling, we may isolate ourselves and withdraw socially. This can lead us into depression. By joining or creating a group, we meet new people. Don't give up old friends, but widen your circle to include more single people.

DATING TO AVOID LONELINESS

When we find ourselves alone, we may be tempted to date to avoid our feelings of loneliness. Often, this attempt to replace our former mate leaves us with less than desirable results. Dating before we've had a chance to evaluate who we are now, and what we want

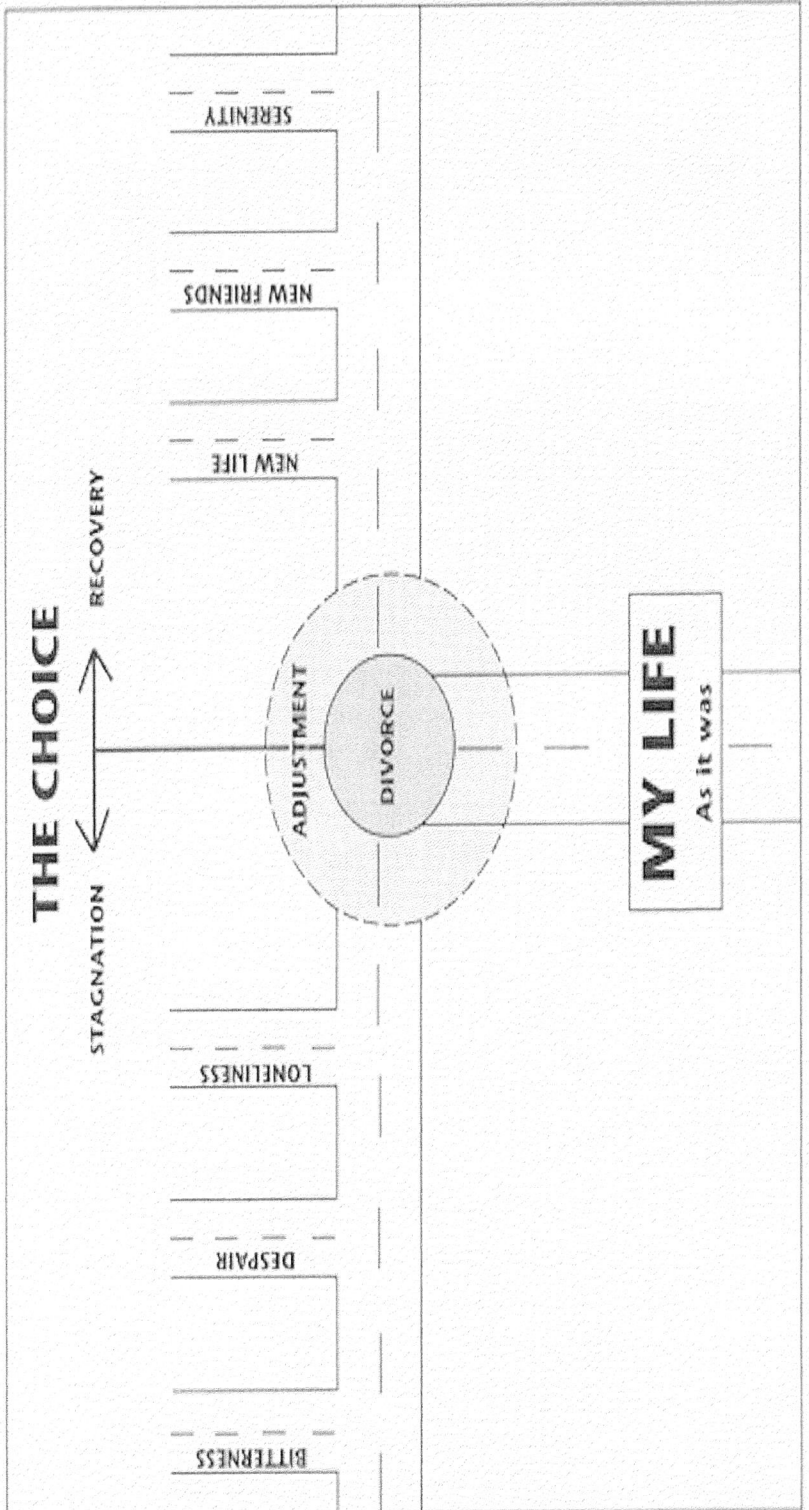

Micki McWade ~ 28

from life, is like trying to hit a target while wearing a blindfold. Instead of evaluating what we need in a relationship, and the self-improvement that must occur before re-entering one, we stumble from person to person, trying to make others fit into the mold of what we want and need. Anything is better than being alone, right? Not so. More often than not, it's better to be alone, at least for awhile. When we take time for re-evaluation, we look at potential partners differently and more appropriately.

Being part of a group dilutes the loneliness by connecting us to others. After awhile, if we have the patience to nurture relationships with those we meet there, we realize that we are not alone. We reach out to people on the phone to talk. We may make arrangements to go out on the weekends and share activities. Members often make plans to go out as a group for a hike, a concert or a dance, for example.

While individual therapy helps us integrate and learn from our experiences, a group provides a different and important level of healing through connection to others. For this reason, many therapists from various practice methodologies recommend a group experience in conjunction with individual treatment.

CHAPTER TWO
ON LEADERSHIP
Understanding What Is and Isn't Our Responsibility

The attitude of the group leader(s) will make or break a group, particularly at the group's inception. While leadership skills are important and will be taught throughout this book, nothing is as important as the warm, caring and non-judgmental attitude of the person who welcomes members into an unfamiliar room.

This warmth and caring shows in our eyes and tone of voice. The group will not coalesce if there's no warmth. Imangine a campfire on a cold day with a group of people sitting around it. If there's no fire, everyone will get cold and leave. In this case, you are the fire. We are not responsible for the well being of a participant but we are responsible for setting a welcoming tone.

If participants feel relief and connection in the group, they are likely to stay. Don't worry, creating a welcoming environment does not fall only on your shoulders. Part of being a good leader is to involve others in keeping the group going and fostering a helpful environment. If the group as a whole is encouraged to welcome new people, they will. The group's well-being comes from having new people arrive all the time. If the group becomes too tight and clique-ish, it will eventually dissolve for lack of new energy.

LEADING AS A TEAM

While a group needs one person who is ultimately responsible, the group will be stronger for having a leadership team, made up of two to three people. We are all good at different things so various strengths create a strong foundation for the group.

The leadership qualities listed here are necessary but can be held by more than one person. While one leader may be comfortable planning a topic and speaking to a group, another may be happier setting up the circle of chairs and being sure that handouts are available. Someone else may feel good about setting up refreshments.

Working as a team provides continuity in the group. If two or three people are committed to being present weekly or bi-weekly, others are more likely to commit along with them. If there's a week where the attendance is small, the team is present and recovery work can still be done within the team. You will likely find that attendance will naturally ebb and flow depending on where group members are in the process, holidays, weather and other uncontrollable factors.

A minimum of two facilitators—a leader and co-leader— also allows for time off and a way to keep the group running smoothly when other life-commitments arise for one of them. As mentioned earlier, the group will become a lifeline for members so it is important that a person with the proper skills is always available to lead the group on the designated night.

An additional advantage of team leadership is that you are ready for growth. Some groups grow to a number where they need to be divided into smaller discussion groups. When this happens, you can split the team leadership between the smaller groups.

LEADERSHIP QUALITIES

What are the characteristics of good leadership? A leader needs to:

- have lived through separation or divorce either recently or in the past. Empathy is an important quality for this work. Stephen Covey, in his best-selling book *The Seven Habits of Highly Effective People* states that the greatest emotional need we have as human beings is to be understood. People come to us in pain and need to feel understood in a group. Although no two divorces are the same and we all take varying amounts of time to heal, having gone through a separation or divorce grants us the ability to grasp the magnitude of the adjustment.

- have gone beyond the shock and pain of the initial separation. In the early stages of separation it's difficult to stay focused and on task. Self-absorption is a normal part of the early adjustment and those in this stage would be too likely to monopolize speaking time. They may not be as empathetic to the other group members because of the inability to look beyond their own pain. This is normal in the early stages, but not good for a group. Someone who is new to the process can be helpful in supportive ways, like making coffee, for example.

- like interaction with people and be comfortable welcoming new members. Usually a group starts off with only a few people so we grow into the role gradually. There will be inquiries on the phone about the meeting so the initial contact on the phone sets a tone for the caller. Calls should be returned promptly and graciously so that the inquiring person feels invited.

- have a sense of humor. Because most groups are open to all, all kinds of people will attend at least one meeting to see if it's for them. No one group will be appropriate for everyone so don't take it personally if some don't return. Bringing some lightness and humor to the meetings is therapeutic for all, but sensitivity to those in pain is important.

There's a fine line between humor and lack of respect. Male- or female-bashing, for example, isn't healthy for a group interaction.

- be able to speak in front of a small group. I found this nerve-wracking in the beginning, but when I understood that group participants were so grateful to have a place to come and to me for hosting the group, I relaxed. I became more and more comfortable as time went by and with the weekly experience.

- be able to speak about yourself to a number of people (usually four to six or so to begin with). One way to start the sharing process is to use ourselves as an illustration, pointing out how we managed an issue. It may be that we managed it well or that what we attempted didn't work. Specific examples of a teaching point are helpful. If we use a story from someone else's life, we need to maintain confidentiality or have permission to share the story.

- be a good listener and stay connected to the person who is sharing

- be able to address problems during the meeting, like stopping crosstalk, for example. Crosstalk (making comments on another person's sharing) is described later in the leadership section.

- be there regularly—and on time. You can, of course, share the responsibility with others on your leadership team. Stable meetings that begin and end on time are generally successful. Because of the tumult of divorce, order is comforting. If the meetings aren't predictable, the group will likely fall apart.

- be responsible for building use, including clean-up and closing. A committee is helpful here, too. We use community buildings like churches, community centers, libraries and sometimes, hospitals for meetings because they are easy to find and their use doesn't depend on one person's availability. We must be responsible and follow protocol in order to use the building long-term. We are all tired at the end of a day and need to pay extra attention to the safety and order of the building we use.

- be able to relate from your experience without getting caught up in it and forgetting that you're leading the meeting. Although speaking about our own experience is necessary for positive illustration, a leader who uses his or her position to monopolize sharing time will undermine the group.

- be strong enough not to date in the group, to avoid gossip and keep the confidentiality of group members. For reasons that will be elaborated on in Chapter Eight, a greater level of maturity is expected of a group leader than of its members. If it's not there, the group is in jeopardy. A leader sets the tone of the group and creates the safety. If members don't feel safe, they don't come back.

- have the humility to avoid judging others. It's a normal human trait to compare and contrast ourselves both positively and negatively with others and there is definitely a temptation to do that in a group setting. It's one way we learn in a group. However, if we spend lots of energy analyzing others instead of ourselves, we miss an opportunity to look at our own shortcomings and grow from that experience.

- have a neat and somewhat business-like appearance at meetings. The leader sets the tone and needs to encourage respect.

Of course, we don't need every quality on this list in order to begin our group. However, we should be aware of our strengths and weaknesses and work on our weaknesses, or look for leadership team members that have those strengths.

These traits also require vigilant monitoring. After leading a group for a period of time, it's easy to forget "the basics". Reviewing these traits regularly or asking a trusted person to let us know if we stepped out of line by talking too much, for example, can help us to quickly correct our behaviors and optimize our leadership. It is important to check in now and then and elicit feedback.

WHAT'S GOOD FOR THE GROUP MUST COME FIRST

The good of the group must come before the personal gain of any individual. The group will not survive if this is not the case. People are very sensitive to a leader's personal agenda and will back away if they feel it's getting in the way of their own progress and rightly so. On the other hand, when a group is going well, everyone gains, including the leader. A successful group grants benefits that can't be achieved alone. A leader or leadership team is in charge of determining the group structure. Having more than one person involved in leadership is especially helpful for this reason.

WHAT'S IN IT FOR US?

Generally, group leaders experience more intense and deeper recovery because they are present at almost every meeting and generally, the more we participate in something the more we get out of it. Facilitators show up prepared, having thought about the meeting topic and perhaps having done some research. The more we learn in order to teach others, the more we enhance our own lives. Doing divorce recovery work not only helps us get through a divorce, it actually enhances our lives. We become more conscious of choices we make and how those decisions affect our lives.

Through group interaction we will learn more about how we affect others. We will become aware of our potential and how to develop it and we'll meet new people and have experiences we wouldn't have had on our own.

Personally, leading a group transformed my life on many levels. Not only did I have a successful recovery from divorce, meaning that I'm happy today, my children are doing well, I understand myself much more than I did—and— I reevaluated my career and literally changed my life. I went back to school, completed my undergraduate degree and went on for a Masters in Social Work. I see myself in a totally different light than I did before my divorce, which is the work of divorce recovery. As a leader, I was there for most of the meetings and the work paid off. This has been true for many others as well.

WHAT ARE WE RESPONSIBLE FOR AS LEADERS?

Our role is to show up, run the meeting and keep it flowing, be respectful and welcoming and take good care of the building we use. What individuals take home is up to them.

We lead by example. Becoming an example is very powerful and the strongest way to convey a message. It is also one of the strongest ways to improve our own lives. If we want people to be on time, we need to be on time. If we don't want destructive gossip going on in our group, we must not gossip. Talk is cheap. People don't listen to what we say unless we are "walking the talk" ourselves.

Talk is cheap.

No one is perfect, but the success of the group depends on our reliability, integrity and maturity as leaders. We set the standard and it's up to us to make it safe for people to share themselves in our presence.

You may be challenged by people who want things done in a certain way, but if the change will affect the entire group, it must be considered carefully before going ahead. We will talk more about handling decisions in Chapter Seven.

WHAT ISN'T OUR RESPONSIBILITY

A group leader or facilitator is not responsible for the recovery of another person. The choice to recover is made by each person who comes in the door. The decision to return, to participate, to embrace the principles, to get better, to let go or to create a new life is up to the individual. No one can do that for anyone else. Some will do really well and others will come to a couple of meetings and drop out. We can't choose for others, we can only choose for ourselves.

Support group meetings are usually peer-led. We do not take on the role of therapist (even if we are a therapist), and we refrain from giving advice at meetings. We aren't aware of anyone's "big picture" so what we say may unknowingly cause more harm than good.

People come to the group, particularly in the early stages, with their own defenses and rationalizations in place. Divorce is a situation that requires people to have a "side" or a story that allows them to go on day-to-day. Rarely are people objective enough to be aware of the big picture. That comes later.

If we believe we have to or are able to solve another's problems, we'll burn out. It's too much responsibility. Even a trained therapist would not attempt to resolve an individual's issues in this setting.

CHAPTER THREE
AN OVERVIEW OF DIVORCE RECOVERY

It is estimated that for every five years of marriage, a person will need one year of recovery. Whether a marriage is good or bad, it creates a strong connection that is deepened over time. A relationship or marriage is an independent entity composed of what goes on between two people. It takes two people to create a relationship and it's made up of the input from those two people. When it's working well, both people contribute to keeping the relationship growing and flourishing.

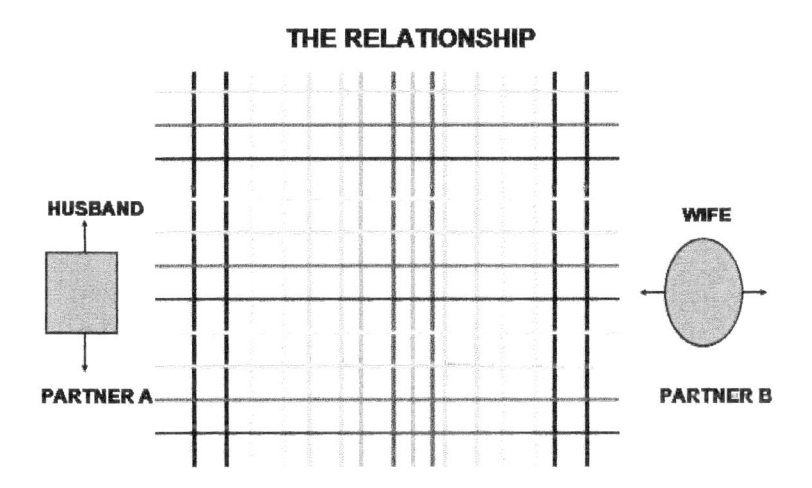

THE RELATIONSHIP

HUSBAND

WIFE

PARTNER A

PARTNER B

Think of the relationship as a piece of cloth. To make cloth, fibers are woven both vertically and horizontally. For the sake of illustration, let's say that the Partner A's contributions are horizontal threads and the Partner B's are vertical. When a relationship begins, the fabric is small, made up of only a few strands. Within a month or two, if things go well, it's woven into the size of a cocktail napkin, for example, and becomes more solid. We enlarge it by introducing each other to friends and family. We share experience, thoughts, feelings, affection and sexuality, allowing our bonds to grow. Months go by and the relationship continues to expand, becoming more important and occupying more room in the life of each person. Think of it as growing to the size of a dinner napkin.

One person can't keep it alive because it eventually collapses without the strong weave going in both directions. This is what happens in many marriages or relationships. One person stops his or her contribution or perhaps both do and what's between them seems to disappear.

As a couple grows closer and the commitment level deepens, the fabric representing the relationship becomes larger and larger. Again, this is made by both people giving time, energy, thoughtfulness and problem-solving ability to developing the relationship.

When a couple decides to commit to each other exclusively, intimacy expands further. Having gone through the introductory stages, worked through some problems, learned to communicate and understand the other person's style, the relationship becomes more and more significant.

When the decision is made to live together, become engaged, marry, have children (in whatever order that may happen) the trust between two people expands with each stage. Roots are set down and the model piece of fabric grows to the size of a small tablecloth. In other words, every time a difference is negotiated, or a deeper commitment is established, another strand is added.

In a long-term relationship or marriage of fifteen, twenty, thirty or more years, the relationship contains a great deal of shared experience. The longer people have been together, the longer it takes to separate emotionally. Again, this is true even if the marriage or relationship was difficult for a number of years.

After twenty-five or thirty years, the relationship illustration grows into the size of a large bedspread. There are so many shared experiences woven into the couple's lives and if there are children, unbreakable connections are present. Dissolving such a relationship requires a dismantling of sorts, almost thread by thread. It can't be torn or cut up the middle. It has to be taken apart slowly and thoughtfully for recovery to take place. Memories continue to surface and good times are remembered, whether we want to remember or not. We may feel like we're on a roller coaster because sometimes we're glad the divorce is happening and at other times grief washes over us like a large wave of the ocean.

We are often startled by the depth of grief we experience because the marriage may not have been viable for a long time. It may have been our decision to end the marriage for many good reasons, so why are we feeling so badly? Even when the divorce is best for all, there is sadness, fear and difficulty with detachment. We may waffle in our feelings about the divorce or breakup and find that very puzzling.

This is a normal reaction to this major transition. The word "transition" is used, rather than "demise" because, when there are children, the relationship will not end. Hopefully, the couple will be able to transform their past relationship into a business partnership, or a less formalized alliance, so that issues with children may be addressed. There will be many future occasions where former partners will be together and it's wise to keep that thought in mind.

People Advise "Move On!"

"Jane, it's been (6 months, one year, three years). It's time to get on with your life! Get over it, find someone else. What are you waiting for?"

Friends and family mean well, but those expectations are unrealistic and don't relate to where a divorcing person is emotionally. Even those who believe they are ready to date soon after separation, usually change their minds after trying the singles scene. That's a hard enough place to be when we're feeling strong, but when we're feeling vulnerable it becomes intolerable. We need ego strength and self-confidence to begin dating.

A support group offers the benefit of others who understand and will not push someone in recovery beyond their limits. There's company without pressure. Emotional recovery work needs to be done before dating makes sense.

WE ARE NOT THE SAME AS WE WERE

A person coming out of a long-term marriage or relationship is not the same as when he or she began it. The experience with the relationship itself, our own maturity level, the stretch we experience by raising children, interaction with our partner's world, including their family and friends have added dimensions to our awareness. There are some things we want to replicate and some we will try to avoid.

We need to ask ourselves "Who are we now?" Will we understand it all right away? No. Reevaluation takes time.

Further, we need to ask ourselves honestly and critically why the relationship failed. We may be tempted to blame our partner completely, but a failed relationship is rarely caused by one person exclusively. How much of the responsibility was ours? We need to assess this and understand our shortcomings to avoid making the same mistake again and again. Perhaps we made an error in selection in the first place.

We are not the same person who entered the relationship, but who are we now? What kind of life do we want? What's missing? What's holding us back? What are our strengths? What can we build on? What are our weaknesses and how can we become stronger? This is the work of divorce recovery and divorce recovery is what takes place in a group setting.

Once there's a good understanding of how we've arrived here in the present, we become ready to move on. A group supports this formative period of personal development—providing a cocoon-like setting for our metamorphosis.

THE POISON OF BITTERNESS

Bitterness is one of the potential and destructive outcomes of a divorce. It's most likely to arise in the partner who didn't want the divorce and has been rejected. The legal system, with the adversarial and sometimes hostile approach, further encourages bitterness. Without supportive people who have experienced the process, a person can get stuck in bitterness and feel the affects on his or her physical and mental health. If we can't get over our bitterness, it has the potential of ruining our lives.

Anger is like taking poison and expecting the other person to die.
—Rabbi Marc Gelman

We need to detach from our spouse or partner in more ways than physical separation. There are ties that bind. When we remain bitter, it's shows that more letting go is necessary.

To return to the fabric analogy, we have to pull these threads out one at a time and unravel what was between us. What we used to rely on our partner for, we now need to do for ourselves. We may be recreating a social life, paying all the bills, becoming a single parent, taking care of the home, preparing meals, removing snow on the driveway, celebrating the holidays differently. These are realizations that come upon us gradually and with each connection that's removed, grief comes up. This is a major life transition.

On the other hand, there is freedom to celebrate and that needs to be realized too. We have choices we've never had before. We no longer have to answer to anyone about how we spend our time or money. We will interact with our children at home without interference, we see friends and family members without having to clear it with someone and our schedules are our own. This feels good.

This evolution can't and shouldn't be rushed. It's an unfolding, like the blooming of a rose. We begin the post-divorce period as a tight bud that slowly and eventually opens to full bloom. It's a natural process that takes time. If it's forced it won't be as genuine or as beautiful. In order for us to come fully into our own, we need to take time to incorporate how this dissolution is affecting us and learn from it. If there is bitterness present the rose will not open.

We don't end bitterness by ignoring it or pushing it aside. We have to go through it by thinking about where we are, how we feel now, grieve the losses, examine our choices in the present and begin to create a new life. Processing all of this takes time and requires support. The longer the marriage, the longer it takes to recover. It takes input from others and willingness to apply new ideas. This is the work of divorce recovery and an effective leader creates an environment where it is safe to open up and come into full bloom because of, or in spite of, the breakup or divorce.

SECTION II

◇

BUILDING A SUPPORT GROUP

CHAPTER FOUR
STARTING A DIVORCE GROUP

In this chapter I will discuss the basics of getting a group off the ground. I have learned a few things in ten years of experience and may be able to save you some time and trouble.

LOCATION

Consistency and stability are important in all aspects of leadership, including location. Finding a location that can be used consistently is one of the first steps in forming a successful group. A home is not the optimal setting for a meeting, because if the homeowner takes a vacation, becomes ill or has a scheduling problem, the meeting has to be cancelled. If the meeting is held in a public building, a co-leader can take over, allowing the meeting to be held in the usual place.

WHERE?

Choose a public building in a central location to which you can give simple directions. You will be giving directions often. A house of worship is a good choice because people feel comfortable going to a church, temple or synagogue for support. Thousands of groups of all kinds meet in church basements, parish halls and classrooms every night of the week. Generally priests and rabbis are happy to have their building used by the community, as long as the property is respected according to their guidelines. The leader is responsible for adhering to these guidelines or assigning another person or committee to the task. It is a good idea to meet with someone within the organization to find out their specific guidelines and preferences for building use. You may want to create a checklist that team members can use to help adhere to these guidelines.

Churches and synagogues usually have chairs, coffee urns, kitchens, coat racks and enough room for a group to meet. Be sure to ask for permission in advance to use the kitchen and equipment. We bring in our own coffee urn, napkins, hot cups, etc.

WHEN?

Schedule a day and time that is mutually convenient for both you and the facility. Again, consistency is important for a successful group and people will expect you to be there. If the meeting is unpredictable, people won't come back. Because our groups have been running for ten years now, we know that people leave and come back, sometimes two and three times. Members also recommend our group to others. Having our meeting at the same place, and at the same time, allows stability for those members who come and go.

ADVERTISE

Obviously a group won't come together unless people know about it. After a while, word of mouth spreads and people discover the group in all kinds of ways. In the beginning, however, it is our job to get the word out.

Announce time and place in local newspapers in the community announcements section. This is usually free.

A sample ad:
A Separation/Divorce Recovery Group will meet every Wednesday evening at 7:30 p.m. The meeting will be held at St. Mark's Episcopal Church, located at the junction of Routes 117 and 133 in Mt. Kisco. All are welcome. For further information, please call John Jones at 555-4321.

- Post fliers in libraries, supermarkets, post offices, churches, etc. Give location, time and date.

- Ask the host church or synagogue to announce the meeting in their newsletter or bulletin.

- Register the group with social service agencies.

- Therapists will also refer people to your group. They know how important it is to be with others in the same situation.

- Matrimonial attorneys may refer to the group

- Many local TV stations have a community bulletin board where they list events and announcements.

Be sure to return inquiry calls promptly. When calls are returned quickly, with a warm, open and friendly attitude, people are more likely to attend. The first phone call sets the tone long before the new person enters their first meeting.

DIRECTIONS

Give accurate directions. People appreciate having exit numbers, distances between turns and other markers so they can find the meeting easily, especially if it is at night. Write out the directions in advance and test them to be sure they are accurate. People are anxious enough when entering a new situation without getting lost on the way. Be sure to include where the meeting takes place within the building—upstairs, basement, Room 201, etc.

ATTRACTING MEMBERSHIP

It's helpful to begin with a few people you know. Ask friends who are going through or have been through a breakup or divorce to join you in starting the group. It's especially helpful if someone has had prior group experience.

If possible, start the group with both men and women. Neither gender wants to walk into a group made up solely of the opposite sex—especially feeling as vulnerable as we do during divorce

Having both men and women in a group helps us understand both gender perspectives of divorce. Men and women cope differently with some divorce issues, while others are experienced in the same way. It has often been mentioned in our group how important it is to hear the opposite sex's point of view from someone other than one's spouse. Defensiveness sometimes precludes communication with our (ex)spouse but when we hear the same words from someone outside our personal framework, we hear it differently.

Having both sexes represented facilitates understanding and stops both male- and female-bashing, which isn't helpful and will only add to the anger that we already feel.

Welcoming newcomers warmly and taking them under one's wing initially is essential. If new members don't feel welcomed and included, they won't come back. If we as leaders can't do it, we ask someone to be a greeter at the door. Some have already experienced tremendous rejection by a partner and will be very sensitive to, and upset by, a feeling of not being welcomed.

Greet people by name whenever possible. A new person returning for a second meeting will feel included and pleased when they are greeted by name. It's worth the effort when you see how pleased people are.

> **Tip:** After the meeting, write down the names and a brief description of the new people and look it over just before you get to the next meeting. It will help you remember and it will mean a lot to those who come back. If I don't remember a name, I say "Tell me your name again. I have to hear it a few times before it registers with me." People don't mind being asked again because they appreciate the effort.

Meeting Setup

You'd be surprised at how important details are to newcomers. You may feel uncomfortable as a new leader, but a divorcing person seeking support for the first time likely feels even more so. It's important to have certain things in place in advance so that you and the members of the group feel welcome and comfortable. The initial impression has much to do with whether or not a person returns.

CONSISTENCY: KEEPING THINGS IN THE SAME ORDER

Divorce creates chaos in many areas of our lives. There's change and upheaval everywhere for awhile so you can understand why consistency and predictability are important elements of support. There's comfort in knowing what's going to happen in general. A consistent format creates a framework that helps members feel secure. There can and should be variety within the framework, but the frame should stay the same. It's what mental health professionals call "a holding environment."

A consistent format will help the leadership too. The set up, the opening of the meeting, the ground rules and the general direction of the group are already established. We just have to plug in the topic for the night. If the regular leader can't be at the meeting, a co-leader or substitute leader will have the format to follow, making it easier on both the substitute leader and the group.

CHAIR SETUP

Set six or eight chairs (or whatever number is ample for your group) in a circle and have more available nearby. Too many empty chairs look forlorn. You'll get a feel for how many you need after a few weeks. Encourage latecomers to sit in the circle. Don't allow anyone to sit outside—it's distracting and seems to pull energy from the group. Try to catch the person's eye and direct them to an empty chair. If there are no empty chairs and the person doesn't know what to do, ask a group member to get a chair for that person. Hospitality goes a long way in making people comfortable and it helps the assisting person feel good too. It becomes clear to everyone that we are expected to help and support each other. This is the way we heal.

Meeting Outline

If your meeting has a regular agenda, a brochure or pamphlet describing that agenda is helpful to newcomers. This brochure can outline ground rules and what to expect at a meeting. Guests can take it home, look it over and begin to feel like they know the format. Place a pamphlet on each chair before the meeting begins. You will find a sample brochure to use as a guideline in the appendix.

Placing several brochures on your information table is also a good idea. Guests and members can share this information with friends. Make sure to include the date, time and location of your meeting in the printed information.

Keep it simple, one page, perhaps printed on two-sides, on regular paper that can be photocopied. Our groups use goldenrod paper because we think it's warmer and more welcoming than white. If you decide to use colored paper, photocopy from a white original. It makes a better copy.

> **Tip:** don't make too many brochures at first. You may decide to make changes after the first few weeks.

HANDOUTS/RESOURCES

People appreciate having articles, ideas, inspiring quotes and slogans to think about and take home as a reminder during the week. Everyone may contribute to the table but we as leaders are responsible for editing what is there. Sarcasm, male- or female-bashing, inappropriate jokes or sexual innuendo are not suitable for this venue. Use your judgment to keep the contents of the resource table appropriate. See Chapter Twelve on resources for ideas.

> **Tip:** We use a plastic file box with a lid and handle from an office supply store to carry meeting supplies like handouts and brochures. It keeps them clean and flat and the file box can be stored in the trunk of the car without spilling. We include a box of inexpensive pens, small sheets of note paper, our phone lists, and the books we use for topics. We tape

the list of emergency numbers to the inside lid of the box.

CHAPTER FIVE
CREATING A SAFE PLACE

PREPARATIONS FOR YOUR FIRST MEETING

Before we host the first meeting, make some general preparations including creating a list of emergency procedures, a support phone list, etc.

It's wise to have a list of emergency numbers in your meeting materials. Generally 911 covers most emergencies like someone becoming ill or having an accident.

CREATING A FEELING OF SAFETY

Our job, in other words, is simply to maintain a safe space for people to share their journey and to be encouraging. How do we do that?

Accept those who come to us with an open heart and mind. People at need to be accepted as they are, without condition. We are often amazed at the growth we see in others and ourselves. Pre-judging someone will cut off an avenue of mutual development. Keep an open mind and welcome the individuality of guests and members.

Refuse to gossip. Trust won't develop if group members think we talk about them when they aren't present.

Be consistent with the meeting format. Those who are going through separation and divorce have enough daily upheaval in their lives and feel better when they know what to expect. Routine creates a feeling of safety.

Remember names. It makes people feel welcome when they are greeted by name. This may take some practice, but it can be done.

Realize that a group leader doesn't have to solve anyone's problems. A self-help group is just that—self-help. Our role is to be there, listen and understand.

SAFE ADVICE

One way we offer advice without doing harm is to have a resource table with helpful information, inspirational quotes and stories, and news about lectures and cultural events. Everyone may contribute to it. In other words, we create an "idea buffet" where people can help themselves and choose the combination that is right for them, or feel free to choose nothing.

If asked for advice directly, speak from your own experience or from a story you know. Give your opinion with the preface "If I were in this circumstance, I would...." Or, "When that happened to me, this is what I did...." Then I conclude with "but you have to do what's best for you." This gives a people something to think about without feeling that they must follow the advice. "You should..." has an entirely different tone. Experience has taught me that people take what they want and leave the rest. This is how we learn best—at our own pace, in our own time.

A visiting therapist commented on the sense of freedom she recognized in the group. The leader is free to interact with people without feeling responsible for everyone's problems, and the members are free to utilize what they need. No one is forcing or resisting. People are free to choose what suits them and will adapt it to their particular circumstances.

SUICIDE THREAT

In the 10-plus years I've been involved in meetings, we have not had this happen, yet we need to know what to do if a person threatens to commit suicide. Suicide is the result of untreated depression. Occasionally a person will say that from time to time they think about killing themselves. It's an idea that goes through his or her mind. This is not a suicide threat by itself and those thoughts are not terribly unusual. However, ask discreetly at the break or after the meeting if he or she is serious or feels that there's a potential for hurting him- or herself.

Generally, groups are anonymous (first-name basis) so once a person leaves the building there isn't much we can do for them unless we have a name and address or know one of their friends. We usually don't have that kind of information readily available unless we know them personally.

If a person says he or she is seriously thinking about suicide and has a plan for how they will do it, there is cause for alarm. The individual needs to get to an emergency room for assessment and help. The police will take a person to the hospital if they are called. Our plan is that one of our leaders will stay with the person and another will call the police. We tell the person that we are getting help for them and stay with them until the police arrive. They will be taken to the hospital. Suicide intervention may save the life of that person.

DOMESTIC VIOLENCE

Also have the number for the closest domestic violence shelter on hand. If a woman reports that she believes her life is in danger, she needs to call the domestic violence hotline in the area for further instruction. People who work these phone lines know how to help a woman in this circumstance. Do not attempt to advise her yourself because there is a specific protocol to follow that will minimize her risk. Most people will not know what's best in this instance and her safety is the prime consideration. Strongly suggest that she call the hotline number.

BUILDING PROBLEMS

In the event something should happen in or to the building, have an emergency contact person to call for building problems.

ALCOHOLICS ANONYMOUS

The Alcoholics Anonymous hotline is another number you might have available. You can find a local number in the business listing section of the white pages of the phone book. There may be someone who comes to the group who is dealing with that problem in their family or in themselves. Divorce creates so much stress that people may turn to alcohol for relief and get into trouble with it before they realize it.

CHAPTER SIX
LEADING A MEETING

The first rule in leading a good meeting is to be yourself. You are one of the members of this group and the more genuine you are, the better. Just be sure that you don't monopolize the conversation. Everyone needs a chance to speak. Our meeting dwindled when one of our leaders couldn't stop talking about her own problems. We as leaders serve the group. It's not an opportunity to pontificate or lecture.

Start the meeting on time. If you decide that the meeting will start at 7:30, start by 7:35. Starting promptly shows leadership and organization, and encourages members to arrive on time.

Again, be consistent with the format. Confidence will grow when leaders and participants feel comfortable and know what to expect after attending a few meetings.

Call the meeting to order by saying something like "Will everyone please take a seat so we can get started." When our meeting was very large, we used a set of chimes to get everyone's attention.

When the group is seated, we open with our format. "We welcome you to our meeting…"

The Meeting Format

Begin the meeting with a moment of silence, because this stops conversations, calms the room and creates an introspective environment.

Write an opening statement that will be read out loud at every meeting. This is what we mean by keeping a consistent format. An opening statement defines the purpose of the group and sets the tone for the meeting. The following is the opening we use:

> We welcome you to the Wednesday night meeting of the Separation/Divorce Recovery Group.
>
> We hope that by being together, by listening to each other, and by sharing our experience, strength and hope, we will learn to see the value of life in a new context.
>
> The purpose of this group is to establish a safe place where we can deal with the pain and isolation brought about by the ending of a significant relationship. We encourage and support those who want to make that ending as peaceful as possible.
>
> We encourage an atmosphere of connection and trust within the group but we are not a singles group or a dating network. Instead, we are a family, where it is safe to be ourselves.

The goal of this meeting is to help us develop into healthier, more complete, independent, loving men and women. We grow by working on ourselves, and by letting go of the focus on others. This is done little by little, one day at a time.

Then we say, "Here are a few meeting rules..."

Note: You may use this at your meeting, modify it or create your own.

MEETING RULES

It's important to tell people in advance how the meeting will be organized and how to conduct themselves in this setting. We include the rules in our brochure or handout. Again, predictability makes people comfortable. New people will enter your group regularly so having your written format on each chair will allow them to get the lay of the land quickly. We read the rules after the opening statement at every meeting. These are the ones we use and they apply to everyone at our meeting:

- What is said in this room is to be treated as confidential
- Everyone will have an opportunity to share

- You may pass, if you wish

- Please don't interrupt people who are speaking with either comments or questions. If you wish, speak to that person at the break or after the meeting

- Please keep your sharing within a five minute maximum. If you go over the allotted time, the meeting leader may interrupt you so that everyone has a chance to speak and the meeting doesn't run late.

ATTENTIVE LISTENING

The most important role we play as support group leaders is that of an attentive listener. We are the receiver of what is being shared. Participants will be sharing deeply personal information so showing appropriate, respectful attention is supportive and necessary. We show we are attentive in a number of ways.

EYE CONTACT

A critical part of the leader's job is to establish eye contact with the person who is speaking. Individuals tend to look at the leader most often when they are sharing, particularly when they are new to the group. If the leader appears distracted or disinterested, the trust level goes down and the speaker becomes uncomfortable. Make sure to look at each person as they speak.

Body Language

The way we present ourselves is noticed, at least subconsciously. It's important to show by our posture that we are alert and interested in what is being said. Specifically, this means that we sit up straight, but not rigidly. Slouching looks disinterested or bored. Keep hands on the lap instead of having our arms crossed, which might look defensive or authoritarian. We might lean slightly forward in the direction of the speaker and use an occasional nod of understanding. When a person is finished speaking, we say "Thanks, Joanne." That's all that's necessary to assure her that she was heard and accepted. At that point we turn to the next person and go on. Everyone is treated in the same way.

Timing

People have different reactions to the various stages they go through in their divorces. Some can barely speak in the early days without becoming extremely emotional so they say very little while others can't stop talking. We believe that it's important for the group as a whole to set a limit on the amount of sharing done by each person. We use a five-minute limit for each person and this is stated in the meeting rules in advance.

This strategy keeps the meeting moving, reduces the chance of one person bringing the whole group down with a long, negative share, and is perceived as fair by the group. Everyone gets equal time if they want it. If there is time left after everyone has had a chance to share, we ask if anyone has something they wish to add. The same timing applies here also.

The exception to this rule is if someone becomes very upset. In our groups we give that person a little extra time. This is a judgment call on the part of the leader. If it seems like the person isn't likely to stop talking by themselves, we gently suggest that he or she stop for now and that we'll talk further to him or her at the break. What works for the group as a whole has to come first. If that's not a priority, the meeting will not survive.

Use the hand signal of a T, or point to your watch to indicate to the speaker that his or her five-minute speaking time is up. If you plan to use this signal, let the group know in advance. If the group is small, time increments can be longer but it's important to keep things moving and give everyone a chance to share.

BREAK-OUT GROUPS

When there are twenty or more people in your group it's wise to divide the large group into two smaller groups. You will need a co-leader to facilitate Group

Two. This gives everyone an opportunity to share without worrying about time running out.

Dividing the group can be done quickly and easily by having people count off by twos. The person next to you starts with one, the next person is two, the next person is one, the next person is two and continue around the circle until everyone is either a one or a two. All the "one's" go to one place and the "twos" go to another. Two groups can work in the same room but it is less distracting if there's a way to separate the groups into different rooms.

CROSSTALK IN A SUPPORT GROUP

Crosstalk refers to side-conversations, argument or discussion of another's point of view during sharing in the circle. When this is allowed, the person who is speaking becomes distracted and uncomfortable and it undermines the feeling of safety in the group as a whole. If one person is disrespected in this way, it affects the whole group because they know they might experience the same thing. On the other hand, respect shown to one member shows respect to the entire group. Encourage respectful and attentive listening to one another. We have heard from many group members that learning to listen more closely without comment has served them well in other areas of their lives.

We are given a defined amount of time each to share our perspective on the topic without interruption or argument. When a person is finished, we all say "Thanks, Mary" or "Thanks for sharing, Joe." That's all. No one is to argue if they disagree with a speaker. Leaders and members don't have to agree with what's being said or personally approve of the individual, but we do have to respect the speaker's thoughts, provided they are shared appropriately. This can be stated in the group from time to time or be part of the group opening statement.

Another reason crosstalk is strongly discouraged is that a conversation can get started between two or three people, leaving the rest of the group uninvolved. Once started, it can go on much longer than you might expect. Crosstalk also creates the potential for defensiveness and may escalate into an argument. The well-being of the group as a whole is our first responsibility and the best environment for a healthy group is a place where we are safe to speak our minds, without fear of argument or attack. Everyone receives the same consideration. You can't go wrong if you keep the whole group in mind—the same rules apply to everyone.

Being heard and shown respect by a group of peers is healing for the speaker (which is everyone eventually) and when progress is reported, we all feel fortified and benefit from exposure to the example. If someone comments on what another said, we need to stop them and say respectfully "Sorry to interrupt, but there is no crosstalk at this meeting. I'll clarify this for you at the break. Thanks."

Speaking from the "I" Point of View

Everyone is entitled and encouraged to discuss his or her own point of view only. "I think (believe, want, etc.) that…" is very different from "You should (need to, have to) do this…. This is an important distinction to practice because we will lead by example on this point. Saying what I believe will help me clarify my own thinking. When ideas are generalized (Everyone knows…, we all think that…) the impact is much less powerful. I can speak definitively for myself and what I believe to be true, but not for the group. Obviously, we all don't think the same way or share the same experience. What is true for me, may not be true for you so I can only state my own interpretation of a topic.

In support groups people learn by listening to one another. We hear examples of what we'd like to employ ourselves and conversely, realize that some ideas would never work for us. We see some members grow and change for the better and some who stay stuck where they are.

> **Tip**: Advise the group to "Take what you like and leave the rest."

Respect for the Individual

A variety of people will come to a meeting and this is good. You'll like some people right away and there will be those you won't like or feel comfortable with immediately. We don't have to like all the participants but as group leaders, we do have to welcome and respect them. I have often been surprised at how my opinion changed about an individual over time. Try to keep an open mind.

Learning to suspend judgment is one of the benefits of group leadership. If tempted to judge someone negatively, ask for guidance from a spiritual source and that you be shown another view of the person. I have been amazed at what that uncovers. In contrast, if I engage in negative thinking, the negative perspective grows. That isn't particularly good for the group dynamic.

People vary in their ability to speak in a group. Some folks will be able to articulate what they think and some will struggle just to say a few words. In an individual's first few meetings, emotions run high. That may also hinder a person's ability to speak. We may not be aware that the person really wants to talk, but is emotionally overwhelmed and chooses to remain silent. As he or she becomes more comfortable this usually changes.

We allow people to pass if they wish. When a person chooses to pass, we say "Thanks, Tom," acknowledging that they are welcome in the circle and we understand.

We must listen to everyone with an equal degree of respect, even if we greatly admire some and don't understand or appreciate others.

BREAK FOR REFRESHMENTS

When everyone has had a chance to share, refreshments can be offered and a group can take a break to chat informally. Ideally a break will last for 15 to 30 minutes, giving people a chance to talk one-one-one or in smaller groups or to ask questions. Providing refreshments, however simple, allows an opportunity for fellowship, and strengthens a group. The break is the time when important interpersonal connections are made. When people feel connected to one or two other members they are more likely to come back and stay on with the group.

Keep it simple. Buy a supply of decaffeinated coffee, sugar, sugar substitute, stirrers, cups and cookies for the break. We recommend decaffeinated coffee because divorcing people have enough trouble sleeping. Milk will have to be purchased every week.

Ask for a volunteer or a few volunteers to take care of refreshments for the meeting. Set up the urn or pot of coffee before the meeting begins so it's ready at the break.

The break is an especially awkward time for new people unless they are taken under someone's wing. If a new person is left standing by themselves, not knowing what to do, they often won't come back. Hospitality shown to a new member will make a person want to come back to the next meeting. A new person needs to be shown the location of the bathroom, where the cups are for the coffee, that there's literature available and other useful information by either the leader or someone assigned to this task. It's a very important duty and should not be underestimated.

New people can fall through the cracks when they arrive with a friend for support. It may seem like they are taken care of, but he or she will need more than one person to feel welcome. Be sure to introduce yourself and some of the other members of the group. Offer to go through the same hospitality routine you would give to any new person who comes in alone. Eventually, this new person will have to come by themselves so having connections with a few people will ensure their connection to the group.

Passing the Basket

Refreshments are paid for from the money in the treasury. One or two dollars a week is collected from the membership to pay for the use of the building and for refreshments. We say, "We have no dues or fees, but we do have expenses." We pass a basket around the circle and collect anywhere from $1 to $5 per meeting, depending on the cost of using the facility.

Some groups end at this point. Our groups have a second section that offers some education. As was mentioned earlier, the first half of the meeting is always devoted to sharing by the group on a given topic. (Topics are covered in detail In Chapter Nine.)

OPTIONAL:
THE SPEAKER AFTER THE BREAK

After the break we often have a more experienced group member tell his or her personal story. They share with others how they have coped and what they have learned so far. This is effective because we listen to people, like ourselves, tell of improvements they have made and we realize that we can change too. A speaker talks for approximately 15 to 20 minutes, or less, about a subject related to divorce or self-improvement. Leave the last 10 minutes of the meeting for questions and discussion.

We may also invite guest speakers. Local professionals like therapists, mediators, psychologists, image consultants, and members of the clergy are often willing to speak to the group, free of charge, on a topic related to divorce. Attorneys, law guardians and mediators are additional possibilities. It's usually good for their practice or business, and the group gets the benefit of their expertise.

It must be stressed to these guests, in advance, that this is not the time to do a commercial for their business. They must be willing to teach the group something useful. The topic can be discussed with you in advance. The speaker may bring in materials like business cards and brochures, but they are expected to be an instructor for 20 to 30 minutes. People can contact them privately if they have been favorably impressed.

Don't be concerned if a few people don't like or aren't interested in a particular speaker. You will not be able to please everyone all the time. Try to have a well-rounded group of speakers so that eventually everyone will find something they can use. Ask members what topics interest them to guide you in your speaker selection. They may also make suggestions.

We've had at least one experience where NO ONE liked the speaker. She sounded good when we interviewed her, but during her talk it became clear that following her own divorce, she was a very angry and bitter person. She used the speaking time to berate her former husband and share her plot to "get him." We all learned from listening to her speak. We realized that we *didn't want to be like her*. That in itself was very valuable to us all. It showed us what we would look like if we took that road and it wasn't very attractive. We were all appalled—a good lesson indeed.

THE PHONE LIST

The phone list is made up of first names and phone numbers and it's an important element in the life of a group. Members are free to add their name and phone number if they wish, but there is no obligation to do so. Obviously, if we are on the list we give permission to people to call us. This list is used to call people if there's a meeting cancellation because of weather or emergency. It's also used to get a group together outside of the regular meeting. One person may organize a hike, for example, and use the list to let others know when and where the event will take place.

Primarily, however, the phone list is used to find support between the meetings. When a person has a need to talk, a group member can find a sympathetic person to listen. We suggest using the phone list when feeling low, lonely or isolated. Etiquette suggests that we ask the person we reach if this is a good time to talk for them. If it isn't we can arrange a time to call back. We continue calling people until we find someone who can take time to talk. We don't have to know a person well to speak with them. We just say that we would like to hear some of their experience, strength and hope for a few minutes. Make sure that people who add their name and number to the phone list understand that they may be getting these calls and are warm and welcoming to the caller, even if they have to schedule a different time to talk.

Our group also has an e-mail list. Jokes, wisdom and notes of encouragement go back and forth all week. E-mail is a way to feel connected to others in the middle of a sleepless night without disturbing anyone. E-mail addresses might reveal last names or employer's names, so this needs to be taken into consideration before a member signs up on the list.

> **Tip:** Yahoo® offers a very easy-to-use, free service, for creating an email group. You can post messages, send newsletters, send e-mail support and even host an online chat in a private chat room. To learn more about this service, visit www.yahoogroups.com

SO, TO REITERATE:

- Start the meeting with a moment of silence.
- Read the opening and the ground rules.
- Go around the circle and have people say their first names.
- Introduce the topic along with how you personally relate to it as an example, remembering to keep it brief. For example: Hi, my name is _____. The topic for tonight is *"One day at a time."* The way I relate to this slogan is that if I think too far ahead I begin to worry. Sometimes I worry so much that I become paralyzed in the present—and the problem I'm worried about may not happen for a long time or maybe not happen at all. I used to get upset and anxious about something that may never happen

and lose today. Now I know that if I take it a day at a time.... For further information, this slogan is discussed in *Getting Up, Getting Over, Getting On: A Twelve Step Guide to Divorce Recovery* on page 118.

- After your introduction, open the meeting for sharing—"Who would like to begin?" Wait for someone to start. Someone always does.

- Work clockwise around the circle after the first speaker.

- People may pass if they wish.

- When people arrive late, they share after everyone else has had a turn, if there's time. They won't be aware of the topic and will need time to catch up. They will become centered by listening to others before they speak. When someone comes in after the sharing has started, and the rotation comes to them right away, say "Because you just came in, Dan, we're going to skip you for the moment and come back to you if there's time." Then turn your attention to the next person in the circle. People understand this move because it's fair to the people who have been waiting for their turn. If the latecomer doesn't get to share because of time constraints, timeliness will be encouraged.

- If there is enough time after everyone has shared, you can get to the latecomers or return to a person who has passed. Members may pass initially but want to speak after they've heard others and gotten some ideas.

CHAPTER SEVEN
DEALING WITH DIFFICULT PEOPLE

Generally, divorce support groups are open to anyone who wants to attend so from time to time, we may have to cope with someone we find difficult. The first thing to determine is whether or not this is a personality clash between you and that person, or if the person is truly difficult. It sometimes takes a few meetings to sort that out.

In my experience, there have been very few people who were truly obnoxious. In fact, I may have found a person annoying when no one else did. That's my first clue that it's my issue and I have to examine that within myself to clear it.

This is an another good reason for having a co-leader or leadership team who will listen to you and give you feedback. It's also good to just vent annoyance on occasion to someone who will not repeat it anywhere else.

Having the meeting rules spelled out in your printed material and read at the beginning of each meeting also helps define acceptable behavior. This cuts down on innocent mistakes that nevertheless interrupt the flow of the meeting.

There are certain behaviors that present problems in support groups. Here are the most common ones.

TALKING TOO MUCH

The most common one of all is talking too long and taking up more than the appropriate sharing time. This can be reduced or avoided by announcing at the beginning of the meeting that everyone has five minutes to share and the meeting leader will interrupt if shares go on too long. Once a person is interrupted a few times, he or she will get the idea and curtail themselves.

Resentment builds in a group if this problem isn't handled. Most people want to share what's going on with them and if one member consistently uses up more time than they should, it becomes a problem for everyone.

I wait until that person pauses for breath and jump in quickly, saying "Thanks for sharing with us tonight, Sue. We need to move on now so that everyone has a chance to share. Finish your thought and we'll go to the next person. Thanks."

During the break or after the meeting I might speak to Sue again and say "I'm sorry to have interrupted you. I hate doing it, but I need to be sure everyone gets their time. Are you okay?"

This shows a little extra concern for her, gives her a chance to respond or ask a question and allows me a chance to restate the policy and that it applies to everyone.

TOO MUCH NEGATIVITY

People come to a support group to feel better which is why I choose a positive or growth-oriented topic to address. Not everyone will be able to address a particular subject because they are too upset and will need to vent. This is okay unless everyone picks up on the "woe is me" tone. If I find that the shares are slowly going downhill, I might reintroduce the topic between speakers, and ask that people point their sharing towards it.

I say "We get together to share our experience, strength and hope at our meetings and to learn new ways of thinking. Why don't we talk about what's going right for us? There are plenty of negatives going on, but there are also good things happening"—or something along those lines. I believe it's my responsibility to keep the tone of the meeting realistic, but with a positive slant. If the meetings become limited to gripe sessions, it does no one any good.

ARGUMENTATIVE PEOPLE

Our groups use the Twelve Steps as topics, but this applies to any kind of philosophy that is used as the platform for your meetings. People who are going through divorce have a degree of understandable anger beneath the surface, and sometimes, it's right on top. They may come into a meeting with a chip on their shoulder and want to disagree with what's being said. They may disagree with the philosophy of the Steps, in our case, or have "a better suggestion" for running the meeting. They may dislike one of our rules. I usually let the person say what they want, unless they go over the allotted time. Again, after the meeting or during the break, I'd say "I heard your objection before and I'd like to explain why we do things this way."

I give a short explanation and if they are still argumentative, I might gently say "This is the way we have found to work best. We understand that the group isn't for everyone. Attendance is voluntary. I hope you'll come back and try it awhile longer. You may get used to our way of doing things while you're here."

Usually, this is a mood and passes by the next meeting, but it's important that the person feel heard and that the issue was addressed, within reason.

Although it remains a challenge at times, I try not to take negative comments personally. They rarely occur because most people are really grateful to have a group, but when they do, I remind myself that I do the best I can and I can't please everybody all the time.

The "Shoppers"

Men or women who come to divorce support groups to find people to date are called "shoppers." The indicators are that either men or women come in obviously dressed up and, in the case of women, made-up for a party. They don't participate in the discussion topic, but insist they are fine and fabulous. ("Then what are you doing here?" I wonder.)

There are others who are members and do the work but are looking to attach to someone as soon as possible. They will approach any new, nice-looking person who comes in the door.

I have a strong objection to this because most people come to a group because they are in pain. The last thing they need is to be forced to fend people off. Their safety is violated by having someone come on to them. This treatment may turn them away from the group because they can't deal with a suitor at that time and don't know how to say "Go away!" nicely.

I will speak to those who consistently go after new people and keep an eye on that situation. If I don't make headway with the person, I'll speak to the new person and suggest that they say a firm "No." because the predator-person does the same thing to everyone who comes in the door.

I believe it's my responsibility to keep the meeting safe. As we read in our opening at every meeting, "This is not a singles group or a dating network, but a family, where it is safe to be ourselves." This is stated right up front.

If people choose to date, it's up to them and I do nothing to interfere. I don't believe it's the best choice in the early days, but I don't attempt to control it either.

PEOPLE SEEKING ATTENTION

There are those who come in occasionally who are very dramatic, who tell wild stories of their past and where and how they are today, seeking the focus of the group. They want an audience. My experience has been that if the same rules apply to them as to everyone else, they will lose interest in the group and eventually drop out.

My style of handling this, although I may be shocked by their presentation at first, is to keep the same expression on my face as always and just say "Thanks, Sam" at the end of their sharing and move to the next person. These people usually don't come to more than two or three meetings if the drama isn't responded to.

THOSE WITH AN AGENDA

Occasionally, someone will want to take the floor to push an agenda. It could be a business idea, a concern for another member and want something done, or they may want the meeting handled in a certain way. This is not to be permitted within the meeting structure. The meeting is a sacred place where people have come to expect the established format. This is part of trust building and healing takes place within it. Those who have an issue to discuss can invite people out for coffee after the meeting to discuss it, but it cannot be done during meeting time.

Making Changes

If there is a legitimate question about meeting protocol and you believe the suggestion is valid, you can always ask for a vote in the group, after thinking about it. It's better to offer choices and vote on each rather than leaving it open-ended. That's why I suggest taking time to think so you can look at options. Any change to be made in group rules or protocol, needs to be made with the entire group in mind. We've had people protest the use of the Steps as our foundation, protest our crosstalk rule, object to one of the co-leaders and lots of other things over the last 10 years. While I am open to new ideas, our group structure is not open for debate, because it works. The success of the group and keeping it going is the most important objective. I feel committed to this.

ASK THE HIGHER POWER FOR GUIDANCE

For those who are spiritual, try asking for guidance with a decision or for dealing with a difficult person. Some of my best ideas and solutions have come from this Source.

CHAPTER EIGHT
DATING IN THE GROUP: RECOVER OR REPEAT

In this chapter we will discuss the dangers of dating in the group as a leader and for the group in general. Some of the reasons are the same and some are different.

We will begin with general information. We know that about fifty percent of first marriages fail, but we need to be aware that 60 to 70 percent of second marriages fail as well. It would be reassuring to think that we learn from our mistakes and second marriages do much better, but that doesn't happen unless we make it so by our own determination. It is essential to the success of later relationships that we understand what went wrong and why. What was our part in the failure of the marriage? What might we have done differently? Maybe the failure was in the selection of our partner in the first place, but if that's true, why did we choose that person? The marital demise may be 80 or 10 percent our responsibility, but whatever it is, we need to understand it. If we don't recover we will repeat the same mistake.

Finding another mate as quickly as possible is an understandable, but unhealthy response to a separation or divorce. Without recovery work, we may settle for the same problem in a different outfit or for a person who is entirely inappropriate for our life today. Second and third marriages are more difficult to navigate because of the hurt and anxiety we carry with us from divorce as well as accumulated life experience and responsibilities in general. We may have children, health or financial problems, we may be taking care of elderly parents and have little time to invest in a relationship. We need to choose wisely and it's not possible without some soul searching about who we are, what we want and don't want today.

The study of metaphysics teaches that we will attract the same person over and over until we learn the lesson that we are meant to learn. We need to take time to understand what has happened so that we don't repeat the same mistakes.

We must take time to evaluate ourselves and our lives and a support group is a vehicle for this work. The meetings are a place where we can focus on our current lives and gain ground by listening to others and giving and receiving support. We don't feel alone and isolated. Working in a group is a expediter and a blessing. Most group members understand that work needs to be done and unlike friends and family who may try to rush us along, those who invest in the group will support each other in the work and the time it takes to do it. For every five years of marriage, it takes a year to get over it. This doesn't mean that we are miserable for years and years, but it does mean that we don't drop all our attachments and feelings because we think it's time to do it. It takes time to work through the process of detachment.

The post-divorce period is a time for healing and reconstruction, for learning and recovery, for strengthening and stretching. It's a wonderful time for self-development and one of the blessings of divorce which we wouldn't have otherwise. Many people, a year or two later, say they are actually grateful for their divorce because of the way they have expanded their lives. This is true for some of us who didn't want the divorce as well as for those who did.

Premature Dating

When we date too soon, and particularly with people in our own support group, we cut off an avenue for this work. Why? Because once we try to impress others with our attractiveness on any level, we stop being totally honest. Our work stops there. If our new love is in the room we won't talk about the misery we sometimes feel or that we still miss our former partner and the familiar situation at times. We're too busy being "cool."

If the new relationship doesn't work out, and most of them don't in the early days for many reasons, it's difficult for people to return to the group. It's too painful. It's embarrassing and awkward to sit in a circle wondering why he or she hasn't returned a call. It's even worse when you see a person you might have dated pay attention to someone else.

We've heard many reports of group members pulling into the parking lot, identifying a particular car and sitting outside for a long time trying to decide whether or not to come in. This creates pain and anxiety and we have enough of that while going through a divorce without adding to it. A participant will certainly not feel comfortable sharing their pain in front of someone they are trying to impress.

On the other hand, We might be separated awhile and think we are ready for a new relationship and notice an attractive, interesting new person. Stop! Not only do we have to determine our own readiness, we have to evaluate a potential partner's readiness too. A newly-separated person may be receptive to attention, but he or she is nowhere near ready for a healthy give-and-take relationship. It is an act of self-sabotage to become romantically involved with a newly separated person. The involvement will delay the new person's recovery as well as our own.

The pink cloud of infatuation is distracting and creates a false sense of security that becomes undone eventually. We all must go through a period of grief and attempt to make sense of what has happened and unfortunately, this cannot be rushed or avoided. Premature romantic attachment delays the natural flow of healing and readjustment, although it appears at first to facilitate it. The divorce recovery work still needs to be done and will undermine future relationships if it is avoided.

We need to mourn the loss of the familiar life we had, understand what part we played in the breakup, determine the changes we want to make in ourselves, help children adjust to the loss of a parent in their home and create a picture of what we'd like our lives to look like. If we go through these steps, we have a better chance of creating a healthy relationship in the future by selecting a more appropriate partner. If we choose not to do this, there is a much higher probability that the next relationship will fail. Not only will we have to cope with the failure of our marriage, but the ending of a new relationship as well. It can become emotionally overwhelming.

When we are dating and infatuated, all the energy goes to that relationship and the deeper, more important work is side-stepped. We need to take time for ourselves. We need to take the time to prepare for the rest of our lives. Select a new partner from a position of strength, not weakness or neediness. This is an extremely important distinction.

There are lots of social groups and ways to meet potential partners. Date there and keep the support group as a place to work and evaluate it. If you begin dating and the relationship is outside of the group you can bring your issues to the group for work. So, if you decide to date, and hopefully that won't happen right away, date outside of the group and work inside.

Serenity is our goal. This promotes physical and mental health—from which we can move on to anywhere we want. The group is a place where we work at achieving that.

Divorce is a gateway to new life! So stop, gather tools and heal. Don't short-change yourself. When dating someone, keep coming anyway. Dating is not a substitute for healing yourself. It's generally a temporary and short-sighted solution.

Go out in groups rather than coupling off to avoid loneliness. Our group members have reported many good times doing hikes, dinners, movies, dances, dancing lessons and more together. You can come and go as you please, have no obligation to anyone—emotional or otherwise—and feel the freedom of choosing what works for you.

DATING AS LEADERS

All of this is true, only more so. We have much more of an obligation to be at the meeting, regardless of who else might be there. We are more likely to use a topic to prove our own point or otherwise manipulate a meeting if we are upset. We must maintain focus on ourselves and the well being of the group. If we are distracted our job is more difficult.

Avoiding this stress is wise. You will have a level of freedom and comfort if you stay neutral with meeting members. With attachment, comes vulnerability.

SECTION III

◇

MEETING TOOLBOX

The following section includes ideas, topics and thoughts for meetings.

CHAPTER NINE
MEETING TOPICS

During ten years of leading groups we have found that having a discussion topic keeps a group from becoming a forum to complain. While there's plenty to grumble about while going through a divorce, listening to an hour or two of negative talk will send people home more depressed than when they came in. Obviously, this is not a healthy support group dynamic and as leaders, we'll quickly wilt from weekly doses of negativity.

Groups vary in their philosophy and focus. Some have prescribed formats, like the Twelve Step Separation/Divorce Recovery Groups or use a book like *Rebuilding*, by Bruce Fisher and work through it. Others don't have a particular focus aside from what is supportive and use a variety of tools. You might choose something from a book, a video, or invite a guest speaker to come in.

The most important aspect of a support group is that people have a chance to talk, to say what's going on with them. Make it a policy to have sharing first and then have the presentation. There are many, many relevant topics to choose from if you know where to look. Many books have been written on the subject of divorce and any of them can be used to spark group sharing. A list of recommended materials is included at the end of this book.

Daily meditation books are also gold mines for topics. *Daily Meditations for Surviving a Breakup, Separation or Divorce* is a book I wrote specifically with this in mind. There are others to choose from and they are generally filled with uplifting themes, quotes and affirmations that can be used as a starting point. In the following pages, you will find ideas for discussion in your group.

Reflection and sharing on the following slogans or statements will be helpful to participants. Think about one of these statements in advance so that you can share first, creating an example for people to follow. Because we have to do this internal work to help others, we find that our progress in our recovery is steady.

Choose one statement, give the group your ideas about it and open the meeting for sharing. These are not written in any particular order. Choose the one that feels right for you that week. If you can relate to it, there will likely be others who need to hear it.

I have collected the following meeting topics over the years I've been leading a group. *Daily Meditations for Surviving a Breakup, Separation or Divorce* and *Getting Up, Getting Over, Getting On: A Twelve Step Guide to Divorce Recovery* contain many more thoughts for sharing in a group setting. You may also sign up for the *Thought of the Day* to receive daily email quotes to think about,

Monday through Friday. That service is free and you can cancel it at any time. Send an email to micki@12stepdivorce.org if you'd like to receive that option.

So if you can't think of a meeting topic, just open up to the day's reading in *Daily Meditations for Surviving a Breakup, Separation or Divorce* (or other daily reading books), read it or have someone else read it out loud and ask who has thoughts on what they have just heard or read. If you keep books with your meeting materials, you'll never be stuck for ideas.

The following pages offer numerous suggestions to get you started. You might also type them up, one per sheet, in large type and have them on your resource table so members can take them home to think about between meetings. We have found them to be very popular and helpful. As you get an idea of what people are inspired by, you will begin your own collection.

Progress, not perfection.

One day at a time.

No matter how daunting the tasks ahead may seem, we only have to take them a day at a time. If our lives seem totally out of control, taking just today and thinking about what we can do in the next few waking hours makes life more manageable. If we want to stop ourselves from doing something, we just have to stop it today—that's all. The present is where our power lies. We may make decisions to change something forever, but today is all that's within our control. One day leads to the next, and if we continue, the new habit will grow just as the old one did.

If we feel down and depressed, we can believe that tomorrow will be different. We just have to get through today. Some of us find it useful to take only an hour or a minute at a time.

AFFIRMATION: Today I won't let myself be overwhelmed. I'll do what I can, knowing that's good enough.

Excerpted from Daily Meditations by Micki McWade (Champion Press, 2002)

Cultivate an attitude of gratitude.

Becoming grateful is the way to happiness. As we're all aware, there are problems to deal with, but often at least 50 percent of our lives may be going well, yet we choose to focus on the down side much more than it deserves.

Melanie Beattie suggests that we look at events differently and reframe them in a positive context. This is not to deny their reality but to expand it. There are many gifts to be received from this practice.

AFFIRMATION: Today I will search for *something* positive in any situation I perceive as negative.

Excerpted from Daily Meditations by Micki McWade (Champion Press, 2002)

If you always do what you always did, you'll always get what you always got.

Repeating behaviors while expecting different results is one definition of insanity. This is a powerful idea. If we want a different result then we have to change something. If we've always been a doormat, it's time to say "No." If we've tried to buy the love of another and it hasn't worked, we need to try a more direct approach. If one tack has been unsuccessful after a number of attempts, it's time to do something different.

Maybe it's time to let go, or stand up for ourselves, or leave a situation. Maybe we need to take action or be patient. Maybe we need to listen to another person's point of view, rather than promote our own side.

This quote contains a powerful idea. Make a change where the same old thing isn't working.

AFFIRMATION: Today I'll see if doing the same thing is preventing me from getting the results I want. If so, I'll choose a different course of action.

Excerpted from Daily Meditations by Micki McWade (Champion Press, 2002)

Love is a verb.

Most of us think of love as a thing—something we want to receive or give away. Instead, think of it as action. We feel unloved during divorce when people who formerly loved us pull away. This may include our spouse, in-laws and friends we had as a couple. We may feel abandoned and lonely.

To get back into the stream of love, do something loving. It can be for a stranger, a friend, an elderly person in a nursing home, a dog at the pound or a friend who is having a hard time. It may be a quick visit or a timely phone call to lend support, or just giving someone a hug. These seemingly small acts may have a profound effect on the receiver and will make us feel better too.

AFFIRMATION: Today I will do something loving for another being without expectation or return, and feel the joy that giving brings.

Excerpted from Daily Meditations by Micki McWade (Champion Press, 2002)

It's okay to look back, but don't stare.

It's important that we understand how we came to our present circumstances. This is always true. In separation and divorce, however, it is possible to spend too much time in the past reliving what happened before.

Usually this stems from fear of the unknown. We look back so we don't have to look toward the future because we are afraid of what we may or may not imagine there. Starting at the past stops us from creating the future in a healthy and constructive way.

Looking back leaves us sad and stuck. Being proactive about our future is what makes life fun and interesting when we get there.

AFFIRMATION: Today I will think about what will make me happy a year from now and work toward that goal a little every day.

Excerpted from Daily Meditations by Micki McWade (Champion Press, 2002)

Three stages in the divorce process when pain is intensified and regression occurs:

- initial separation,
- legal process
- finding that your ex-partner is in a romantic relationship.

Say what you mean, but don't say it mean.

We can and should express our opinions, but we don't have to beat a person with a club to get our point across. There's a big difference between stating our preferences or views and attacking another person verbally. Demeaning words are very destructive and hurtful. What's more, nothing positive is accomplished by them.

Children are especially affected by meanness. Their self-esteem is diminished when a parent says negative things about who they are. For example, there's a difference between; "You are a bad child" and "I don't like the way you are acting." In times of high stress we need to be very careful of how we speak to people.

Monitoring ourselves is our responsibility, regardless of provocation.

AFFIRMATION: Today if I feel the need to defend my self, I'll evaluate whether it's really worth doing or if I can just let it go.

Excerpted from Daily Meditations by Micki McWade (Champion Press, 2002)

I have decided to stick with love. Hate is too great a burden to bear.

—Martin Luther King.

Come to the edge, Life said. We are afraid, they said. They came, It pushed and They flew.—Unknown

While living through divorce, it's natural to be afraid. So many major changes take place. Change, however, can push us to new heights that are undreamed of now.

Not only do circumstances change, but *we* are also transformed. It's up to us to create wonderful new things for ourselves—to learn to fly solo. For those who have been married for many years, being alone may seem bleak and lonely at first, *but* it's also an opportunity to explore our ideas and needs, and redefine our reality. Believe it or not, this may turn out to be a positive experience.

Many people who were devastated by their partner's leaving and have been on their own for a few years wouldn't choose to go back to their marriage. They have created a new sense of self and prefer life in the present to what it was in the past.

AFFIRMATION: Today I will have faith that I will be able to fly when necessary.

Excerpted from Daily Meditations by Micki McWade (Champion Press, 2002)

Argue for your limitations and sure enough, they are yours.

—Richard Bach, *Illusion*

Between stimulus and response, man has the freedom to choose.

—Viktor Frankl

When we are upset and agitated we commonly react too quickly. This statement reveals the importance of thinking before responding. Regardless of how we are provoked, we are responsible for our choices, and we will have to answer for them. Learn to take a deep breath and think before reacting. There will be enough to apologize for while moving through separation or divorce, without adding to the list.

AFFIRMATION: Today I will pause to take a few deep breaths before reacting to negative stimulus. I will choose my reaction wisely.

Excerpted from Daily Meditations by Micki McWade (Champion Press, 2002)

On Being Yourself

You must learn that you cannot be loved by all people. You can be the finest apple in the world—ripe, juicy, sweet, succulent and offer yourself to all. But you must remember that there are people who do not like apples. You must understand that if you are the finest apple and someone you love does not like apples, You have the choice of becoming a banana. But you must be warned that if you choose to become a banana, you will be a second rate banana. But you can always be the finest apple. You must also realize that if you choose to be a second-rate banana, there will be people who do not like bananas. Furthermore, you can spend your life trying to become the best banana—which is impossible if you are an apple—or you can seek again and be the finest apple!— *Author Unknown.*

I've Learned...

That it is best to give advice in only two circumstances: when it is requested and when it is a life threatening situation.

—Andy Rooney

POSITIVE ATTRIBUTES
A FOURTH STEP INVENTORY
Progress, not Perfection

I am learning to love myself; learning to trust God; learning to trust other people; seeking help when necessary; asking for advice from positive people; telling the truth; speaking from the "I" point of view; saying what I mean but not saying it mean; being open to love others; able to draw boundaries; saying no when it's necessary; not pleasing others when it's harmful to myself; saying yes to life; forgiving others; understanding that lack of forgiveness hurts *me* most of all; being responsible for my serenity; being responsible for my feelings and subsequent actions; following through; keeping my word; listening to others—without becoming defensive, thinking about what I'm going to say, or adding my own biography; apologizing when necessary; being courageous but not abusive in the face of confrontation; being able to diffuse, not exacerbate a difficult situation; being able to put the children first; respecting their grieving process and being supportive of them; refusing to put another down when everyone else is doing it; doing a good day's work and feeling satisfied at the end; learning to smile often; having a kind word for others, even if I'm not feeling too great myself; being patient, non-judgmental, happy and nice to be around; having an interest in my appearance; seeking to be part of the solution, not part of the problem; being able to avoid talking just to hear myself talk; being able to admit when I don't know the answer; being able to admit that I was wrong, instead of making excuses for myself; seeking growth and maximizing my potential; realizing that I am capable, sincere, well-meaning, reliable, timely, creative and that I have many gifts, some developed and some yet to be discovered. I have learned to take one day at a time, to let go and let God, and I am willing to practice turning things over to a Higher Power even when I doubt there is anyone listening.

Micki McWade, Twelve Step Divorce Recovery

To shame the parent
is to dishonor
the child.

—Mark Bryan
The Prodigal Father

Time

Imagine there is a bank that credits your account each morning with $86,400. It carries over no balance from day to day. Every evening it deletes whatever part of the balance you failed to use during the day. What would you do? Draw out every cent, of course!

Each of us has such a bank. Its name is TIME. Every morning, it credits you with 86,400 seconds. Every night it writes off, as lost, whatever of this you have failed to invest to good purpose. It carries over no balance.

It allows no overdraft. Each day it opens a new account for you. Each night it burns the remains of the day. If you fail to use the day's deposits, the loss is yours. There is no going back. There is no drawing against the "tomorrow." You must live in the present on today's deposits. Invest it so as to get from it the utmost in health, happiness and success! The clock is running.—*Author Unknown*

Make the Most of Today.

- To realize the value of ONE YEAR, ask a student who failed a grade.

- To realize the value of ONE MONTH, ask a mother who gave birth to a premature baby.

- To realize the value of ONE WEEK, ask the editor of a weekly newspaper.

- To realize the value of ONE DAY, ask a daily wage laborer with kids to feed.

- To realize the value of ONE HOUR, ask the lovers who are waiting to meet.

- To realize the value of ONE MINUTE, ask a person who missed the train.

- To realize the value of ONE SECOND, ask a person who just avoided an accident.

- To realize the value of ONE MILLISECOND, ask the person who won a silver medal in the Olympics.

- Treasure every moment that you have! And treasure it more because you shared it with someone special, special enough to spend your time.

I am indebted to the anonymous author of this wonderful writing.

**Some people are in our lives for a moment,
some for a season
and some for a lifetime.**
—Iyanla Vanzant

CHAPTER TEN
TWELVE STEP SEPARATION/DIVORCE RECOVERY GROUP MEETING FORMAT

The Twelve Steps are the backbone of our Separation/Divorce Recovery groups. They were written by Bill Wilson in 1938 for Alcoholics Anonymous and have been used by thousands of groups of all kinds since then. The reason they have been so effective is that they are a "blueprint for living," combining common sense with spirituality in clear and simple language. They have been used to help people transform their lives in ways that individuals never thought possible, and yet, the program is entirely doable.

You might wonder how the Steps that are used to move away from an addiction might be useful in divorce. There are enough similarities between the two problems to make this solution viable. The philosophy, plus working with others for inspiration and support, works very well for separating from the familiar way of life.

Divorce/Addiction Recovery Comparison
A Major Shift

Addiction: Dependent on substance
Divorce: Dependent on person

Addiction: Lots of habits related to substance
Divorce: Habits & daily life around spouse

Addiction: Culture based around habit
Divorce: Culture based around couple-life

Addiction: Friends are in that culture
Divorce: Friends are usually part of couple life

Addiction: Affects finances
Divorce: Affects finances

Addiction: Children may be neglected
Divorce: Children may be neglected

Addiction: Can't imagine life without…
Divorce: Can't imagine life without…

Addiction: May blame others for problems
Divorce: May blame others for problems

Addiction: Creates chaos and unmanageability
Divorce: Creates chaos and unmanageability

Addiction: Giving up substance creates crisis
Divorce: Giving up relationship creates crisis

Addiction: Impacts all levels of life
Divorce: Impacts all levels of life

The Twelve Steps have been used in many contexts and their use is expanding all the time. One of the advantages of using this format is that it attracts those who are already familiar with the program. Therapists recommend these groups to their patients because they are comfortable with the well-known, straight-forward philosophy.

Getting Up, Getting Over, Getting On: A Twelve Step Guide to Divorce Recovery describes how the Steps can be applied to divorce. That book is available at all major retailers like Barnes & Noble and Borders, and through Champion Press at www.championpress.com and from Amazon.com.

Chapter Four of that book outlines how to lead a Twelve Step Divorce Recovery Group. The following is an excerpt from that chapter.

Begin the meeting with a moment of silence and follow with the Serenity Prayer.

God, grant me the serenity
to accept the things I cannot change,
the courage to change the things I can
and the wisdom to know the difference.

Read the opening and the rules from your meeting format, and have everyone read the Twelve Steps together. People will get to know them on a weekly basis.

Start the discussion with an overview of why the Twelve Steps are an effective way to deal with divorce—something like...

We use the Twelve Steps because they have proven over the last 70 years to be useful in dealing with change. The Steps are best known in the field of recovery from addiction. Giving up an addiction means a change in priorities, relationships, social conditions, job status, sleep patterns and so on. The changes divorce precipitates are very similar. Through the use of the Steps, we are able to transform ourselves during this time of upheaval and change, and the changes we make now will alter our lives in ways that we can't even imagine. The Steps keep us focused on ourselves and the choices we make as we cope with and adjust to our new situation. If we practice the Twelve Steps we will see that we heal, adjust and move on with hope, integrity, self-confidence and self-respect.

Then choose a step or slogan to talk about. As a leader, you will have to introduce the subject. If you have no experience with the Steps, read some material from *Getting Up, Getting Over, Getting On* aloud and then discuss the ideas you've read. There are many other resources to draw upon for new ideas on practicing the Steps. A bibliography has been placed at the back or Chapter 12 of that book for that purpose and there are "Recovery" as well as "Divorce" sections in most bookstores.

After your introduction, it works well to ask who wants to start the discussion and work clockwise around the circle after the first speaker. People may pass if they wish.

We have found that having the Steps as a weekly focus reduces our work by having the sequence of Steps as our opening topic. We talk about a Step or a slogan every week as our meeting opener. We cycle through them time and time again and find that each time we talk about one, there are new ways to relate to it. This is true in all kinds of Twelve Step groups—the Steps are our guiding principles. They are listed here in outline form for your information.

Step One: *We admitted we were powerless over others [alcohol] and our lives had become unmanageable.* When we recognize that we cannot control another person, no matter how smart, articulate, convincing we may be, we put more time into our own lives—where it belongs and can do the most good. We can only control ourselves, our actions and reactions. We may be able to influence by example, but we cannot force a person to do what we want them to do. By spending our precious time and energy trying to control, manipulate and seeking revenge, our own lives become unmanageable because we aren't taking care of ourselves and developing our own potential.

Step Two: *Came to believe that a power greater than ourselves could restore us to wholeness [sanity].* Some of us turn to spirituality during crisis and think of the power greater than ourselves as God. Some of us will go to a therapist, some will read helpful material, and some will join a group. The main idea is to be open to outside resources to help you through the crisis. Studies have shown that those who have peer support recover faster and more fully than those who are isolated. Joining a divorce support group speeds the recovery process because we gain support and learn from each other—and don't wear out our friends and family members.

Step Three: *Made a decision to turn our will and our lives over to the care of God as we understood God.* The Twelve Step program is a spiritual one. We learn by practicing the Steps to connect in a real way with our Higher

Power. While the program is spiritual, it does not espouse any particular religion. Also, it's not necessary to be religious to find help in the program. An open mind is enough. We do the best we can and then turn the outcome over to the care of God, asking for wisdom, courage and guidance in making the many important decisions that are necessary during this process.

Step Four: *Made a searching and moral inventory of ourselves.* It is important to assess our strengths and weaknesses after a marriage or long-term relationship ends. We are not the same as we were when we entered the relationship. We need to understand where that leaves us now and decide which characteristics to eliminate and which to nurture. Awareness is the first step.

Step Five: *Admitted to God, to ourselves and to another human being the exact nature of our failings [wrongs].* When we admit to God, we are forgiven, when we admit to ourselves and take ownership of our failings, we begin to see that change is possible. When we admit to another human being, we realize that we are human—no more, no less. No one is perfect and everyone makes mistakes. By admitting them, we take the second step in making significant change. Be sure to choose a supportive person to talk to.

Step Six: *Were entirely ready to remove these defects of character.* This Step sounds deceptively simple. "To become ready" may involve letting go of a long-held stance. We may have to stop a destructive habit. Look at a behavior or characteristic you want to give up and decide what the opposite might be. Rather than beating ourselves up for having the characteristic, it's more advantageous to focus on what we *want* instead. You may want to replace impatience with patience, for example.

Step Seven: *Humbly asked God to remove our shortcomings.* When we get to the point of having seen our shortcomings, talked about them and decided that we don't want to repeat them in the future, we have done a lot of good work. What we may not anticipate is how difficult it is to break old habits, so this is where Step Seven is helpful. We don't have to do this alone! When we ask God for help, we get it. We will be supported in making the personal changes that will lead us to a better life.

Step Eight: *Made a list of all persons we have harmed and became willing to make amends to them all.* We might put ourselves at the top of the list! Have we neglected our health or are we using alcohol or drugs to get through this? Are we allowing ourselves to become exhausted by constant running or malnourished by eating junk food instead of a healthy meal?

Our children suffer during the divorce process. Are we doing our best to see that their suffering is minimized? Are we using them as weapons against our (ex)spouse? Do we burden them with our problems, rather than talking to a friend or therapist?

Step Nine: *Made direct amends to such people, except when to do so would injure them or others.* Many times an apology is all that's necessary. Other times, we need to change our behavior or break a habit. Before taking action we need to evaluate whether we are doing this step from genuine remorse or in an attempt to manipulate a situation. Sincerity is a key factor. And remember, making amends won't be worth much if we continue to do the same thing.

Step Ten: *Continued to take personal inventory and when we were wrong, promptly admitted it.* Apology, like humility, is vastly underrated. Some think that to apologize is to admit weakness, but the opposite is actually true. To apologize promptly creates freedom from thinking about excuses and justifying why we did something. As long as we're alive, we'll continue to make mistakes but isn't it easier to trust a person who can admit when he or she is wrong, than someone who always needs to be right?

Step Eleven: *Sought through prayer and meditation to improve our conscious contact with God, as we understood God, praying only for knowledge of His will for us and the power to carry that out.* Prayer is asking and meditation is listening for the answer. Both of these practices are very helpful during divorce. This is something we can do for ourselves and is within our power. We might pray for strength, wisdom and guidance on a particular problem, and the courage to make the necessary changes, rather than holding on to the past. We all have our list of issues we need help with.

Step Twelve: *Having had a spiritual awakening as a result of these steps, we try to carry this message to others and practice these principles in all our affairs.* If you practice these steps as you go through divorce, people will ask you how you managed to get through it without becoming stuck and bitter. It's at that point you explain the tools that you used. It's also enormously helpful to study the Steps with a group who are experiencing the same kind of difficulty. Being with others really helps.

No matter where we are today, or what our circumstances may be, every one of us has enormous potential for creating a better life. Taking the time to recover and discover the *you-of-today* will pay big dividends as you move forward. As we say in the Twelve Step movement, "It works if you work it, so work it—you're worth it!"

After everyone has had a chance to share on the opening topic, we take our break for coffee, tea and some cookies.

When the break is finished, we sit back down in the circle and have an additional discussion. We present a speaker from either inside or outside the group or we choose another subject to talk about. This second part isn't mandatory. You can end the meeting after the refreshments if you want a shorter meeting. Ours generally lasts 90 minutes to 2 hours.

CHAPTER ELEVEN
Essays by Group Leaders

Laurie S.
Twelve Step Divorce Group Leader

Being a group leader has been one of the most positive, liberating, and self-expanding experiences of my life. Let me backtrack:

I joined Micki's group in June of 1997 when I was newly separated, shell-shocked and scared to death. My dear friend, Laura, dragged me to my first meeting where I heard the message that divorce can be the beginning of a whole new life, if you choose to believe it and do the work. That was exactly what I needed to hear. I had been hearing so many negative messages about divorce. I was feeling rejected and like a leper in my upscale community of "perfect families". I grabbed onto the idea of "first day of the rest of your life" as if it were a matter of survival, and it was for me.

My ex-husband wanted out and as hard as that was to deal with, somehow I knew I was being set free to find out who I was. I didn't know who I was and I had been afraid to find out. I was a wife and mother and those roles were important to me. I love my kids dearly but I knew there was so much more to me and here was my chance to find out.

My support group is a Twelve Step Separation/Divorce Recovery group. It took a while for me to understand the Twelve Steps but they gradually became part of my being. I live my life according to them now and they always lead me to what I need. The philosophy put me on a positive path and I have become a much more spiritual person through the program. Don't get me wrong, I was suspicious of what I thought might be a "cult-like" mentality for a while, but I always remained open. I'm glad I did.

I became a break-out group leader at a large meeting for a while and then Micki suggested I start my own group in another part of our county. I struggled with that decision for a long time. I still had tremendous fear issues of stepping out on my own. I had a wonderful therapist who helped me sort out my feelings and find the strength to do it. It took a lot for me. I was again in a place where I needed a lifeline. I had to try it. I owed it to myself.

My group was be four years old in April 2004! It has been my anchor. It has given me so much and I am so grateful to have it in my life. I want to mention a few things that have really helped me. First, I found two wonderful people, Sharon and Mary, to help me right from the beginning. They are loyal, dedicated and supportive and I surely couldn't do it without them. We all worked together to find a place to meet, to select our guest speakers and almost everything else. It was and is a shared effort and joy. I was scared in the beginning and I still get a little nervous sometimes, but that's me. My main word of advice is to be who you are, be authentic. I believe we are our best when we are authentic and it gives other people permission to be who they are.

There are times I feel like I don't know what to say and I think I sound stupid. I remind my self that this is not a performance. I am not there to be brilliant. I am there to help people and I do that by being as authentic as I can. If I don't understand a Step, I'll be honest about it. I am one of the group. We all learn from each other. The other thing I believe is that this group and the Twelve Steps, helps people help themselves and we do that "by sharing our experience, strength and hope".

> Twelve Step Divorce Recovery Group
> Church in the Highlands
> Bryant Avenue, White Plains, NY
> Monday nights 7 to 9 PM

Elizabeth S.
Former Leader of Twelve Step Divorce Group

I will write something, even though I'm not sure of my writing skills, because being a leader has been such an advantage to my everyday life especially as an addictions counselor.

Being involved with this Twelve Step Divorce and Separated group has made me feel very strong and confident about my own divorce. Many times I sat with all my fears of being alone, unable to reach out to someone who really understood how hard it is. This is where the group was very supportive. By leading a group I was carrying the message that life really does go on. I wanted to make people feel safe and not judged. It's very important to be a good listener.

I have learned to keep the focus on myself, knowing the only person I can change is me. I try to learn something instead of making the same mistake over and over again and thinking the outcome has to be different.

The tone of the meetings has always been people helping people, and that making change is a process and done over time. I always believed that certain people were put in my path for a reason.

What has always helped me run a meeting is telling my story. I always believed that someone in the circle would relate to it somehow and not feel so alone.

Lois Czajkowski
Divorce and Beyond Support Group,
St. Bernard's Church Bridgewater, N.J.

God calls people in strange ways. Some five years after I was divorced, I attended Mass at my parish church, St. Bernard of Clairvaux, in Bridgewater, N.J. In the weekly bulletin was an advertisement for someone to lead a group for separated and divorced Catholics. Even though I was working as a teacher, raising my two children, and caring for a sick mother who also lived with me, I responded to the call. When I was going through my divorce, there were no groups around that I was aware of, and I had to go through all of that pain alone. To this day, I don't know how I got through it.

I went for training at a half-day session sponsored by my diocese, took voluminous notes, and met other people who were also in training. Upon completion of my training, my parish sent a letter to other parishes explaining that I was starting a group at St. Bernard's, and asked them to put the information in their Sunday bulletins. That was five years ago.

Our groups have taken a variety of formats, although we always start with a prayer. Before we used to discuss almost any topic that participants brought up, but now we use the book *Divorce and Beyond*, by James Greteman, C.S.C. and Leon Haverkamp, M.S.W. Our ongoing group uses its follow-up, *When the Trust Breaks* by James Greteman. Sister Jacquelyn Donohue, I.H.M., our Associate for Parish Spirituality and Adult Formation, now acts as a co-facilitator with me. Sister Jackie has a variety of materials from which to choose. Besides using the books, we have guest speakers. So far we have had counselors, attorneys, a canon-law lawyer who addresses annulments, a social worker, a published author, and a variety of speakers to assist group members get through these very trying times.

Our meeting begins and ends with a prayer. At the initial session people introduce themselves by first name only and briefly tell about their situation. Topics such as the process of divorce, self-image, stress, anger, blame and guilt, loneliness, growth forgiveness and happiness are discussed. The books we use offer structure for the program and suggest questions to be answered during the meeting and later at home.

Because of the success of the groups, we also meet during the between meetings. Some people choose to come back after their nine-week session ends and others move on. At the present time our on-going group meets once a month, while the beginners meet the other three weeks.

We usually have a holiday gathering at a local restaurant. Some members get together in small groups and go to singles' dances, to the movies, to play miniature golf, and to dinner. We try to cover all aspects or a person's healing.

> **Lois Czajkowski**
> Co-Facilitator
> Divorce and Beyond Support Group
> St. Bernard's Church, Bridgewater, N.J.
> Wednesdays, from 7:30 to 9 pm
> 908-725-0552

Beth O.
Former leader Twelve Step Divorce Group

Although I no longer facilitate a Twelve Step Divorce Recovery group, I do have a small group at work that meets twice a month. There were so many staff members who would come to me to share that it just naturally evolved. I do share the Twelve Steps informally and once again have to go buy Micki's book, *Getting Up, Getting Over, Getting On: A Twelve Step Guide to Divorce Recovery*. This will be my 4th copy! I lend it out and never get it back! Anyhow, here goes...

Facilitating a support group was pivotal in my own personal healing process. Where better to share your inner most feelings but in a non-judgmental, caring, been-there-done-that atmosphere. The hurt and the anger are understood by each and every group member. Although each of our stories are different, they're all the same. The characters and events may differ, but the feelings of rejection, anger, sadness and sometimes hopelessness are palpable within the group.

Leading a support group by facilitating a meeting can often be a challenge. Each person has their own agenda and their own need to share, to vent. The dynamics of each meeting are amazingly different, depending on the participants of that group. Reviewing the rules at the beginning of each session is vital for a successful meeting.

As a facilitator and a member, who needs to get as much from the meeting as the others, it's important to lead without being the "counselor." I always let it be known that I have no answers, no easy way to get through this difficult period, but that I struggle right along with them, side by side. I think it's necessary to convey this message before each and every meeting. The format of having each member speak without interruption is also important for stress reduction and for the success of the meeting.

Following Micki's book, *Getting Up, Getting Over, Getting On* provides the structure of the meetings: taking each Step and applying it to our own specific situation are the skills we need to cope. Working on these skills is often how we get through each day.

I remember my very first meeting, thinking, "I don't have these problems—it's him!" *He* needs to come here, not me! How naive; how revealing! I look back now and have to smile. In the beginning the hurt is so overwhelming it's hard to think that I have to work on me. After all, the other one is the one who caused this! Enter the Twelve Steps, the tools that assist our painful but necessary journey toward healing.

There were times at meetings when someone's pain was at such a surface level, I needed to gently help them end their "tirade" so another member would have their chance to speak. These times were difficult but manageable. Interrupting them and being honest as to the time constraints of the meeting, yet understanding their need to share, allows the meeting to continue. It was important to let them know we as a group, would be willing to listen during break or after the meeting ended. Allowing the member one more minute for closure would ease them out of the spotlight and allow the next member to begin sharing.

Listening to one sad story after another could at times be discouraging, yet I would come away from each meeting feeling more like "I can do this, I'm not alone, I'll be ok." I think remembering these meetings are proactive in your determination to not just get through the difficult period, but get through it with a sense of honor and wholeness; this is what makes this program so successful. Leaders need to subtly allow that hopefulness and the feeling that there is a life after separation and divorce to permeate the meeting.

I'm grateful I had the opportunity to facilitate a group and meet all the wonderful, dedicated leaders make up the Twelve Step programs. I'm still in touch with four members from my own small group and they will be life-long friends. We have shared the best of times and the worst of times with each other and "we're still here".

If God brings me to it, He'll bring me through it… but meanwhile it's nice to know there's a safe place to go and share the disappointments and hurts along the road to recovery.

Sally F.
Twelve Step Divorce Recovery Group Leader

I knew I was ready to lead the group when the words "I'll do it" came out of my mouth one day with no hesitation. Until then I had been a co-leader with on-and-off responsibilities, which suited me just fine.

This is the first time I've given thought to what changed, and it's clear to me what did: my urge to give back became stronger than my need for support.

Anyone who moves up from regular Joe to management knows that things irrevocably change, and the same goes for a support group. Even though ours is a Twelve Step group, one way we differ from AA and Al-Anon, for instance, is that the leadership position isn't a rotating one. With us, once a leader always a leader—so it's a big responsibility to take on.

I also was following Micki, who started our group and had led it for nine years. Gulp. But, as I said, I was ready or I wouldn't have accepted. It took a few months though before I felt like the leader in a real sense.

It's been almost two years now. I'm comfortable enough that I rarely get nervous before meetings. I also try to remember that the Steps really do take care of themselves—we are just the delivery mechanism. That's why AA and other Twelve Step meetings don't need permanent leaders to be effective. Just providing a place and time to think and talk about the steps is enough. Keeps me humble, too.

Here are some stray thoughts on my leadership experience so far:

- I try to act like a leader, even on nights when I don't feel like it. This means being on time, being prepared, and summoning my concentration and compassion.
- I really keep an eye on new people. I'm trying something where, at the end of going around and saying our first names, I re-introduce newcomers and say it's their first meeting. It's my way of cueing others to talk to them at the break. I remind myself how nervous I was walking into a meeting for the first time.
- When I introduce a Step, I make a concerted effort to reach back to my earlier experiences in recovery

so I can relate the Step more to people in the beginning stages.
- I do a quick recap of the Steps up to the one we're working on if that night's group is made up of fairly new or brand-new people.
- New people have a tendency to arrive early, so I give them a job right away—setting up chairs, putting leaflets out, helping with the coffee. I introduce them to other people as they arrive.
- I resist my inner people-pleaser and confront people when they consistently break the rules, i.e., interrupting others, speaking too long, speaking off the topic, preaching (too much "you" and not enough "I"). I may have to do this privately but I do it.

Over the ten years I've been in the group, I've heard numerous people say that they always feel better leaving the meeting than they did when they came in—and many add that often those are the nights they really didn't want to come in the first place.

As a leader, the same thing happens to me. There isn't a night I don't drive home feeling better than when I got in the car to come. And on top of that, I know there are others driving home who feel the same way—and I had something to do with it.

The rewards are great. When I was asked to lead the group, it was like accepting an invitation to grow. It was scary, but that "yes" was pretty close to the surface. I feel the growth every week, and I meet it head-on. That feels good.

Mary P.
Twelve Step Divorce Group Leader

I have been separated for five years, divorced four years, and have been a break-out group leader for three years. My experience as a leader has been one of the most rewarding of my life, knowing that I am performing a much needed service to people who are in emotional pain. At the same time I know that I serve as an inspiration and give hope to people who are just beginning the long journey through their divorce.

For me, the most important thing that I do as a leader is to listen carefully and to be positive about the future. People in the group come to be heard, and in speaking their thoughts aloud, they experience healing.

I believe that it is important for leaders to recount their own pain when he or she first joined the group, even though they may have completed the healing process, in order to help newer members realize that divorce can be an opportunity for improvement.

My experience as a leader has taught me that everyone, without exception, has something to offer. I have absorbed a bit of wisdom from every person who has come to group, and I am forever grateful to all of those people for their part in my growth.

> Twelve Step Divorce Recovery Group
> Church in the Highlands
> Bryant Avenue, White Plains, NY
> Monday nights 7 to 9 PM

Elsie Radtke
Coordinator for Divorce and Annulment Support Ministries
Family Ministries Office, Archdiocese of Chicago

I coordinate divorce ministry for the Catholic Archdiocese of Chicago and in this capacity, oversee 30 divorce peer support groups. I provide clergy education to acquaint priests and deacons with the need for divorce ministry, help parishes select leaders to facilitate divorce ministry groups, and train prospective leaders to deliver effective ministry. I also enrich them in the work they do in the parishes and clusters.

I mention this background because divorce ministry and healing have become very important elements in my adult life. I never expected to do this sort of work. I never thought I would ever be divorced. It has been a challenge to listen to what God has asked of me and to follow that call. Divorce ministry was what I needed to become involved in to find my voice and my value in the world after years of struggle to maintain my marriage.

When I was first divorced and tried to find a divorce support group, all I encountered were groups that were cliquish and judgmental. There was a competition in the groups I attended for who could complain the most, who had the hardest life, and who was wronged most grievously. It was dreadful. Other groups I attended were "meet" markets. It was very scary to walk into a group hoping to get some understanding and some help managing this loss in my life only to find these kinds of situations.

In the years of doing divorce ministry work, I have learned a lot. I have learned that we are all good people. I have learned that the end of a marriage can be the start of a new life of spiritual insight and generosity of heart. I have learned that divorce ministry was the "growing up" piece I needed to move beyond the pain and embarrassment of my own divorce. I have learned that in participating in divorce ministry we can learn how well we are healing, or not. I have learned that it takes a long time to get over the end of a marriage. It takes about five years! I have learned that divorce ministry taught me to accept the limits of my humanity. A group is successful if its leadership consider themselves "facilitators" rather than "experts." Each of us has a shared experience, yet it is also unique. We need to allow the people who come to the groups to heal in their own time.

People who have had the experience of divorce are best deliverers of divorce ministry. However, many who divorced long ago, are not suitable to participate in divorce ministry leadership as they often forget how it felt to be newly divorced, plus, the causes and effects of divorce today are somewhat different from 10 or 20 years ago. Likewise, newly divorced people are not suitable for leadership because they are still too raw and not healed. They need to be helping themselves, not others. This leaves the most likely candidates for leadership to people who have been divorced more than a year but probably not more than seven to ten years.

Divorce group leaders must receive training. They need to be taught skills to facilitate group discussion so that all who attend will have the chance to participate and be heard. The format of Twelve Step meetings has a good history of success in this regard. It assures that there are no "experts" and the wisdom of the group provides a healthy and safe environment for divorce recovery. The trainer teaches clear guidelines for the group to follow that give structure and order to the group and allows it to flourish and carry on regardless of who is in the leadership positions. In this way the responsibility for the group is shared.

I have seen people in divorce ministry who never leave the group. It became a safe place for them and they felt welcomed and understood in the group. It becomes the definition of who they are. The group becomes their "new" partner in life. I would hope that not many of us want to go to our grave with that distinction. There are a few people I have encountered who have been in the ministry for a very long time and are still contributing in a healthy way. These folks are very few, though.

Managing a group requires great sensitivity and openness. Of particular concern are the people who come to a group hoping to meet their next mate. This must be discouraged as it creates the wrong environment in the meeting place. The purpose of the group needs to be clearly defined to be a healing outreach after divorce that address the spiritual needs of the participants. While the desire to socialize is evident in this ministry, it is a separate ministry and must be set aside as such. A divorce recovery group might meet once a week for two hours and only do divorce recovery work. A second gathering once or twice a month at a separate place and time might be warranted for those who would like to dance or eat or study some other book or interest. Keep them separate. Participants will not feel that they are compelled to date if they are not ready. All will be free to attend as much or as little of the activities offered as they wish.

It has been my experience that divorce ministry is not for people who are separated. It is for people who have filed for divorce or are in the process of divorce or who are already divorced and seeking recovery. People who are separated need a different kind of help to examine what sort of separation they are involved in and how they might proceed in the relationship. They need help to rebuild the marriage with professional help or they need individual help to manage the personal issues presented in the marriage. They need encouragement to stay with the marriage and learn skills to retrieve the original love and commitment that they made the day they wed. They also need help to move towards divorce if that is the only wise recourse.

Finally, in ministry we must be mindful that it is never about us. It is about the people of God and their pain. We are called to walk with them a while and we must do no harm. We can listen, we can nod, and understand. We need to keep our stories to a minimum and share our strength received in our own recovery. It is a blessed and holy opportunity we have been given. We must always honor that.

May God bless you in your ministry and recovery.

Elsie Radtke
Associate Director
Coordinator for Divorce and
Annulment Support Ministries
Family Ministries Office
Archdiocese of Chicago
www.familyministries.org

Pat F.
Twelve Step DSA Group Leader, Nassau County, NY

Leadership is the ability to see the long view. It is the ability to have a view of yourself, to be able to view your group as a whole with you in it, and to make decisions for the whole, based on past experience and hope for the future.

True leadership has no room for egotism, nor does it include selfish goals. Good leaders are responsible, trustworthy, committed to and have a passion for the topic, and are excellent listeners. They are not controlling but can maintain order. They are genuine, grounded and are respectful of others.

Good leaders display a sense of self-worth, belonging, expectancy, responsibility, accountability and a sense of equality. Leaders take a strong role in developing, expressing and defending civility and group values.

Effective leaders have a deep intuitive sense, they continue to develop and listen to that intuition. They wait for it to come forward as they are making their decisions.

Only those groups that have a strong leader will develop into meaningful and stable ground for work to continue and deepen. A fully developed group will model for its members a sense of intimacy as experienced in intimate relationships. They feel accepted and whole, even with their faults and defects. They are listened to and have learn to listen to others without criticism. They have hope for better relationships in the future. Only the brave souls who feel the need to change and feel safe to develop that change will keep working at it.

So, to sum up, true leaders offer hope, encouragement and safety. As a long and committed leader of a divorced and separated group, I have developed some values for myself and my relationship to the group members. Some of those values are keeping a polite distance in social situations, I never date anyone in the group or track anyone down when they don't show up for awhile.

What I've learned
About Becoming Too Involved

About five years ago, a man called about his desperate marital situation and his near suicidal emotional state. I kept close phone connection with him until the night of the group when he showed up. Unkempt, unshaven and distraught, he cried and told us his story. We listened. We understood. We empathized. He came back, week after week.

He tried many times to act normal and contribute in conversational tones. He eventually sought professional help and took anti-depressant medication. Gradually, he came alive and his focus became me for awhile. He thought I was wonderful and placed me on a very flattering pedestal. He wanted to be my friend, did everything for me, held the door, put the chairs out, made the coffee, offered to help in other ways, changed my flat tire, called in the evenings to see if I needed help with anything.

I found myself feeling rosy all of a sudden, needy and adolescent. He sat next to me when the group went to the diner after the meetings. He parked his car next to mine in the parking lot and walked in with me. I was confused by this and at the same time felt wonderfully valued.—and, it semed, I was falling in love.

When the group met and I sat in the circle, I never forgot that I was the leader and responsible for the health of the group. I had my own values and was especially committed to the responsibilities of leadership.

He tested me every week with his bouts of comedy, crosstalk and acting out. I maintained my composure. He continued to pursue me and I mistakenly continued to act as his therapist and best friend, with the relationship going nowhere.

When I was in my right mind I knew he wasn't capable of an intimate relationship at this stage, yet I found myself hoping something would happen between us.

He eventually started dating—not me, of course—but other people in the group when he fixated on them and would sit next to them in the diner. He still declared me as his best friend. On and on it went. One day I realized that he hadn't called in weeks and at the next meeting I approached him and asked why he never calls his "best friend." "Friends are supposed to pay attention to each other," I said. His anger erupted and I fell off the pedestal.

I was very relieved in the end, but it hurt too. I remained cool and calm whenever I saw him, which was weekly at the meetings. He continues to come to the group to this day and still pursues new women. He never called me his best friend again.

It was a very interesting experience and I learned a great deal from it. For a time it was very nice being idolized and yes, he did help me heal some things from my past relationships. So what did I do for him? He continued to grow and develop, is still coming to the group and is still involved in his therapy.

Beware of admirers in your group. They will teach you many lessons.

My role as a leader centers me, connects me with my spirituality and gratitude every day. I am in awe of this ability to lead and have people stop and listen to me when I start to speak. I never take advantage of the people I lead. I reach out for their hands and touch their hearts as they touch mine. I am on sacred ground sitting in a group and I thank God every day for allowing me to be there. I thank everyone for showing up to share their specialness and resiliency and for allowing me to witness their growth. How lucky I am!

Carole S.
Twelve Step Divorce Group Leader

I had a desire to bring a Twelve Step Divorce Recovery Group to South Florida. My thought was that, regardless of whether only one other showed up, the idea would be worth pursuing for that person and for me. The thought of applying the concept of being "powerless over others" is genius!

Having facilitated this group for approximately one and one half years, I have experienced tremendous growth, as well as watched those in the group do the same. The size of the group has ranged from 2 to 20, with about 7 or 8 steady members. Those coming more often remark to each other how far they have seen each other come—from tears to smiles. The group has been thanked over and over again for the support and wisdom with which most members have been blessed. Outside the group, between meetings, many members call each other for individual support. The entire experience has been priceless! Each group generally ends with an expression of gratitude from each member, the most familiar being "I am grateful for this group."

> Carole Staigle
> Friday nights 7:00pm
> Delray Beach Community Center
> 50 NW 1st Avenue 561 637-6622

CHAPTER TWELVE
A Leaders Checklist

In advance

- The room is booked for a convenient time for you
- The announcement of time and place has been placed in the local papers
- Directions to the meeting location have been checked and are written out
- Potential members have been contacted and inquiry calls have been returned
- A supply of decaf coffee, sweeteners, milk or powdered cream and a bag of cookies (optional) is in place

Right before the meeting

- Be at the location at least 10 minutes before the start time
- The chairs are set in a circle, unless you'll be seated around a table
- The meeting format has been placed on the chairs
- The coffee is on so it's ready at the break
- Someone is prepared to greet people as they arrive

- Handouts are on the resource table (optional)
- Your topic information is handy
- You have a basket or container to pass for the weekly contribution
- Start the meeting within 10 minutes of the designated start time

During the meeting

- Call the meeting to order with a moment of silence
- Read the opening statement from the format
- Have everyone say their first name around the circle
- Introduce a guest speaker, if there is one
- Introduce the topic
- Open the meeting for sharing, remembering…
    ~eye contact
    ~attentive expression and open body language
    ~say "Thanks, _____." when a person is finished speaking
- When everyone has had a chance to speak, pass the basket for donations
- Invite people to have coffee at the break
- Have someone show new people where the bathrooms are

After the meeting

- Make a fast note about names so you remember them
- Ask for help putting the chairs away and cleaning up the coffee service
- Make sure the facility is picked up and left in good order
- Check that coffee pot is unplugged and clean
- Double check that the doors are locked and the lights are out if that is part of your responsibility
- Great job!

CHAPTER THIRTEEN
SAMPLE BROCHURE

SEPARATION/DIVORCE RECOVERYGROUP

Getting Up, Getting Over and Getting On

Below is a sample of the text we use in our meeting brochure.

WELCOME...

We welcome you to the meeting of the Twelve Step Separation/Divorce Recovery Group.

We hope that by being together, by listening to each other, and by sharing our experience, strength and hope, we will learn to see the value of life in a new context.

The purpose of this group is to establish a safe place where we can deal with the pain and isolation brought about by the ending of a significant relationship. We encourage and support those who want to make that ending as peaceful as possible.

We encourage an atmosphere of connection and trust within the group but we are not a singles group or a dating network. Instead, we are a family, where it is safe to be ourselves.

The goal of this meeting is to help us develop into healthier, more complete, independent, loving men and women. We grow by working on ourselves, and by letting go of the focus on others. This is done little by little, one day at a time.

Here are a few meeting rules —

- What is said in this room is to be treated as confidential.
- Everyone will have an opportunity to share.
- You may pass, if you wish.
- Please don't interrupt people who are speaking with either comments or questions. If you wish, speak to that person at the break or after the meeting.
- Please keep your sharing within a five minute maximum. If you go over the allotted time, the meeting leader may interrupt you so that everyone has a chance to speak and the meeting doesn't run late.

We have chosen and adapted the Twelve Steps of Alcoholics Anonymous and Al-Anon as the basis of our recovery program because we know that this format works and that these principles have helped many people before us. The Twelve Steps promote spirituality, not religion. Let's read the Steps together.

The Twelve Steps

1. We admitted we were powerless over others — that our lives had become unmanageable.

2. Came to believe that a power greater than ourselves could restore us to wholeness.

3. Made a decision to turn our will and our lives over to the care of God, as we understood God.

4. Made a searching and fearless moral inventory of ourselves.

5. Admitted to God, to ourselves and to another human being the exact nature of our failings.

6. Were entirely ready to have God remove our defects of character.

7. Humbly asked God to remove our shortcomings.

8. Made a list of all persons we had harmed and became willing to make amends to them all.

9. Made direct amends to such people wherever possible, except when to do so would injure them or others.

10. Continued to take personal inventory and when we were wrong, promptly admitted it.

11. Sought through prayer and meditation to improve our conscious contact with God as we understood God, praying only for knowledge of His will for us and the power to carry that out.

12. Having had a spiritual awakening as a result of these Steps, we tried to carry this message to others and to practice these principles in all our affairs.

IN CLOSING...

In closing, we would like to say that the opinions expressed here were strictly those of the person who gave them. Take what you liked and leave the rest.

The things you heard were spoken in confidence and should be treated as confidential. Keep them within the walls of this room and the confines of your mind.

A few special words to those of you who haven't been with us long: if you try to keep an open mind, you will find help. You will come to realize that there is no situation too difficult to be bettered and no unhappiness too great to be lessened.

We aren't perfect. The welcome we give you may not show the warmth we have in our hearts for you. After awhile, you'll discover that though you may not like all of us, you'll love us in a very special way—the same way we already love you.

Talk to each other, reason things out with someone else, but let there be no gossip or criticism of one another. Instead, let the understanding, love and peace of the program grow in you one day at a time.

THE SERENITY PRAYER

God, grant me the serenity
to accept the things
I cannot change;
the courage to change
the things I can;
and the wisdom
to know the difference.

WORDS OF WISDOM

Recover or repeat.

If you always do
what you always did,
You'll always get
What you always got.

Develop an
Attitude of gratitude.

One day at a time.

BIBLIOGRAPHY AND OTHER HELPFUL RESOURCES

The general idea of this list is to provide lots of different approaches to feeling better. All of these books provide inspiration and creative ways to enhance one's life. They all provide ideas to talk about.

A Course In Miracles. Triburon, CA: Foundation for Inner Peace, 1975. A study of forgiveness and an interesting teaching on miracles.

Ahrons, Constance, Ph.D. (1994) *The Good Divorce: Keeping your family together when your marriage comes apart.* New York: Harper Perennial. A classic on divorce, explaining possible options in relationship with ex.

Albom, Mitch. *Tuesdays with Morrie.* New York: Doubleday, 1997. A series of interviews with a man who is dying. Great teachings on how to live life.

Bach, Richard. *Illusions: The Adventures of a Reluctant Messiah.* New York: Dell, 1977. Lessons on how we create our own reality and choices we have.

Ban Breathnach, Sarah. *Simple Abundance: A Day Book of Comfort and Joy.* New York: Warner Books, 1995. A daily reading and reminder that there's a lot to be grateful for.

Beattie, Melody. *The Language of Letting Go.* New York: Harper Collins, 1990. An excellent daily reading on letting go of others and focusing on ourselves.

Beattie, Melody. (1996) *Codependent No More (2nd Ed.).* New York: Hazelden Education Information. A definition of codependency and suggestions on how to change old ways.

Buscaglia, Leo F. Loving Each Other: The Challenge of Human Relationships. New York: Fawcett Books, 1990.

Carlson, Richard. *Don't Sweat the Small Stuff...and It's All Small Stuff.* New York: Hyperion, 1997.

Carlson, Richard. *Don't Sweat the Small Stuff at Work: Simple Ways to Minimize Stress and Conflict While Bringing Out the Best in Yourself and Others.* New York: Hyperion, 1998.

Campbell, Joseph, Bill Moyers. *The Power of the Myth.* New York: Bantam Books, 1991. Description of archetypes and how they apply to life at various times.

Chopra, Deepak. *The Seven Spiritual Laws of Success: A Practical Guide to the Fulfillment of Your Dreams.* San Rafael: New World Library, 1994. Interesting way to bring more abundance into our lives. Each law can be a discussion topic.

Clapp, Genevieve. (2000) *Divorce and New Beginnings.* New York: John Wiley & Sons. Excellent overview of divorce and all the stages we live through.

Covey, Stephen R. *The Seven Habits of Highly Effective People.* New York: Fireside Books, Simon and Schuster, 1990. A classic on how to make most of everyday while enhancing relationships. Each habit can be a discussion topic.

Dass, Ram. *Still Here: Embracing Aging, Changing and Dying.* New York: Riverhead Books, 2000. Author has had catastrophic stroke and makes the most of what he has.

Fisher, Bruce (1996) *Rebuilding: When Your Relationship Ends* (7th Ed.). San Louis Obispo: Impact Publishers. This book is used by many Catholic groups and has positive approach to getting through divorce.

Frankl, Viktor E. *Man's Search for Meaning* New York: Simon and Schuster, 1959. Incredible true story of survival and growth while in a Nazi concentration camp.

Hahn, Thich Nhat. *Peace is Every Step: The Path of Mindfulness in Everyday Life.* New York: Bantam, 1991. Simple, gentle, wise readings.

God's Little Devotional Book for Women. Tulsa: Honor Books, 1996. Good discussion topics.

God's Little Devotional Book on Success. Tulsa: Honor Books, 1997. Good discussion topics.

Hay, Louise. *You Can Heal Your Life.* Santa Monica, CA: Hay House, 1984. A study on how our emotions affect our health.

Kubler-Ross, Elisabeth M.D. (1969) *On Death and Dying.* New York: Macmillan. Originally written to explain stages of preparation for death, but now used to understand grief of any kind. Divorce creates a death of a relationship and will be mourned like deaths of significant family members.

Major, Jayne A., Ph.D. (1994) *Creating a Successful Parenting Plan: A step by step guide for the care of children of divided families.* New York: Harper Perennial. Suggestions for making workable parenting arrangements.

McWade, Micki, CSW (1999) *Getting Up, Getting Over, Getting On: A Twelve Step guide to divorce recovery.* Beverly Hills: Champion Press. Explanation of how the Twelve Steps and slogans apply to divorce.

McWade, Micki, CSW (2002) *Daily Meditations for Surviving a Breakup, Separation or Divorce*. Fox Point Wisconsin: Champion Press. Daily readings to help the reader through this type of adjustment.

Neuman, Gary, LMHC (1998) *Helping Your Kids Cope with Divorce the Sandcastles Way*. New York: Random House. Excellent book on helping children through divorce. Practial suggestions and developmental information included.

Noel, Brook. Klein, A. (1998) *The Single Parent Resource*. Beverly Hills: Champion Press, Ltd. Good ideas and suggestions for single parents.

Oriah Mountain Dreamer. *The Invitation* San Francisco: Harper, 1999. A wonderful, inspirational reading for meeting topic.

Pine, Arthur, Houston, Julie. *One Door Closes, Another Door Opens: Turning Your Setbacks into Comebacks*. New York: Delacorte Press, 1993. More things to think about.

Robbins, Anthony. *Giant Steps*. New York: Fireside, 1994. Moving on and getting busy with new goals.

Robbins, Anthony. *Personal Power II: The Driving Force*. Robbins Research International, Inc. 1996. Motivational material for moving on.

Tagore, Rabindranath. *Fruit Gathering*. Asia Book Corp of America, 1985.

Rodegast, Pat and Judith Stanton. *Emmanuel's Book*. New York: Bantam Books, 1987. Wise metaphysical writings.

Shimberg, Elaine F.(1999) *Blending Families*. New York: Berkley Books. Information on how to raise a stepfamily.

Tannen, Deborah (1990) *You Just Don't Understand: Women and Men in Conversation*. New York: William Morrow & Co. Outlines communication differences and difficulties between men and women.

Thoele, Sue Patton. **The Woman's Book of Courage: Meditations for Empowerment and Peace of Mind*. Berkeley: Conari Press, 1996. Daily meditations for women.

Thoreau, Henry David. *Walden*. 1854. Current Edition: Philadelphia: Running Press, 1990. Classic book on awareness of the present surroundings.

Trafford, Abigail (1992) *Crazy Time*. New York: Harper Perennial. Great description of the difficult days of early separation. Makes one feel normal.

Vanzant, Iyanla. **One Day My Soul Just Opened Up*. New York: Fireside, 1998. Inspirational reading on many useful topics. Again good subject matter for meeting topics.

Wallerstein, Judith S., Lewis, J. M., Blakeslee, S. (2000) *The Unexpected Legacy of Divorce*. New York: Hyperion. Report on 25 years of research on the effects of divorce on children.

Walsch, Neale Donald. *Conversations with God: An Uncommon Dialogue, Book 1:* New York: G.P Putnam's Sons, 1996. Uplifting spiritual material.

Williamson, Marianne. *A Return to Love*. New York: Harper Perennial, 1993. More uplifting spiritual ideas.

Kabat-Zinn, Jon. *Wherever You Go There You Are Mindfulness Meditation in Everyday Life*. New York: Hyperion, 1994. Reminds us to be conscious of our life on a daily basis.

Index

Item	Page Number
Addiction	128
Admitted to God...	133
Advertise	55
Agenda	92
Alcoholics Anonymous	67
Anxiety	23
Apology	135
Archdiocese of Chicago	152
Argue for your limitations	116
Argumentative people	89
Attentive listening	72
Attitude of gratitude	108
Attracting membership	56
Bach, Richard	116
Becoming too involved	158
Bedspread	45
Being on time	36
Being yourself	118
Big picture	41
Bitterness	48
Blueprint for living	127
Body language	73
Breakout group	74
Bryan, Mark	122
Building Problems	67
Burn-out	41
Business partnership	46
Calls	34
Chair set-up	59
Change in group	93
Children	20
Children	25
Children	113
Children's mental health	25
Co-leader	32
Come to the edge	115
Company without pressure	47
Comparing to others	37
Confidentiality	37
Confidentiality	66
Consistency	59
Consistency	64

Critical choice	26
Crosstalk	35
Crosstalk	75
Critical Choice	26
Daily Meditations for Surviving a Breakup,	104
Dating	27
Dating	46
Dating as leaders	100
Dating in the group	95
Day and time	54
Defects of character	133
Depression	23
Detachment	49
Detachment	97
Difficult people	87
Directions to site	56
Dividing the group	74
Divorce and Beyond	143
Divorce is a gateway	100
Divorce ministry	152
Divorce Support	19
Divorce/Addiction comparison	128
Domestic violence	66
Email list	83
Entirely ready	133
Essays by group leaders	139
Evolution	47
Eye Contact	72
Fabric analogy	43
fabric, cloth	44
Facilitators rather than experts	153
Failings	133
Fear of the unknown	111
Feedback	38
Fisher, Bruce	104
For every five years…	43
Fourth Step inventory	120
Frankl, Viktor	117
Freedom	49
Friendly attitude	56
Friends and family	96
Fruit Gathering	176
Gelman, Marc	49
Getting Up, Getting Over, Getting On	129
Giving advice	41
Giving people hope	151
Good for the group	76
Good listener	35

Gossip	64
Greeting people by name	64
Greteman, James	143
Grief	46
Grief	50
Guest speakers	144
Guilt	22
Handouts/Resources	61
Healing process	145
Hospitality	60
Hospitality	80
House of worship	53
Humility	37
Humility	134
Humor	34
If you always do…	109
Illusions	173
Impatience	134
Infatuation	98
Insanity	109
Inventory	133
Issues we need help with	136
Keep an eye on new people	149
Lawyers	24
Lead by example	40
Leader responsibility	31
Leaders checklist	163
Leadership qualities	33
Leadership team	37
Legal system	48
Listening carefully	151
Location	53
Loneliness	100
Love is a verb	110
Made a list	134
Making the most of today	124
Martin Luther King quote	114
Matrimonial attorneys	56
Medical perspective	23
Meeting brochure	167
Meeting format	70
Meeting outline	60
Meeting rules	71
Meeting topics	103
"Meet" markets	153
Men	21
Men and women in a group	57
Metaphysics	96

Napkin	44
Negative group	23
Negativity	90
New social circle	27
Next mate	156
One day at a time	84
One day at a time	107
Overview	43
Passing the basket	80
Peer-led	41
People helping people	142
Personal development	48
Personal inventory	135
Phone list	82
Positive attributes	120
Post-divorce period	97
Posture	73
Power greater than ourselves	132
Prayer	136
Prayer and meditation	135
Premature dating	97
Progress, not perfection	106
Progress, not perfection	120
Qualifications	13
Rebuilding	103
Recover or repeat	95
Refreshments	79
Rejection	22
Relationship illustration	43
Responsibility	31
Responsibility	36
Responsibility	41
Responsibility in marriage	46
Rewards	151
Roller coaster	45
Rooney, Andy	119
Rose	49
Safe advice	64
Safety	63
Safety in the group	76
Sample ad	55
Say what you mean	113
Self-absorption	34
Sensitivity	34
Sensitivity and openness	155
Serenity	100
Serenity Prayer	171
Seven Habits of Highly Effective People	33

Shame	122
Sharing Process	35
Shoppers	91
Shortcomings	48
Shortcomings	135
Sincerity	135
Speaker	81
Spiritual awakening	136
Spiritual program	133
Starting promptly	69
Step 1	131
Step 2	132
Step 3	132
Step 4	133
Step 5	133
Step 6	133
Step 7	134
Step 8	134
Step 9	135
Step 10	135
Step 11	135
Step 12	136
Stepping out on my own	140
Stick with love	114
Stimulus and response	117
Strengths and weaknesses	144
Successful groups	20
Suicide threat	65
Supportive community	19
Talk is cheap	40
Talking too much	88
Team leadership	32
Telling my story	142
The Prodigal Father	122
Therapist	41
Therapists	55
Thought of the Day	104
Time	123
Time off	32
Timing	74
Tip	20
Tip	22
Tip	58
Tip	77
Tip	39
Tip	61
Tip	84
Transition	46

Treasury	80
TV stations	56
Twelve Step Divorce Groups	103
Twelve Step Divorce Groups	127
Vanzant, Iyanla	126
Walking the talk	40
Welcoming environment	31
What's in it for us?	39
When the Trust Breaks	143
Wholeness	132
Wilson, Bill	127

Daily Meditations:
For Surviving a Breakup, Separation or Divorce
MICKI MCWADE, MSW

Micki McWade, MSW, introduced a new form of support for those surviving the loss of a relationship with her book *Getting Up, Getting Over, Getting On: A Twelve Step Guide to Divorce Recovery.* In *Daily Meditations for Surviving a Breakup, Separation or Divorce,* McWade offers daily nuggets of support, wisdom and encouragement to guide people on their journey. Compassionately written, each entry is sure to enlighten, encourage and touch the reader. This second book is derived from McWade's *Thought of the Day Program*—an internet e-mail group she maintains to send daily words of support.

Getting Up, Getting Over, Getting On:
A Twelve Step Guide to Divorce Recovery
MICKI MCWADE, MSW

Borrowing the wisdom gained in the development of 12 Step Programs, *Getting Up, Getting Over, Getting On: A Twelve Step Guide To Divorce Recovery* offers learned and proven support. For over 50 years, 12 Step Programs have helped millions of people work through difficult and painful situations. Now, these 12 Steps can help the many Americans who are left pain-filled after a divorce. Author Micki McWade adapts the best techniques, information and life-lessons of long established recovery programs, to provide a concise and comprehensive pathway toward a fulfilling life after divorce. Whether during the painful days of the divorce itself, or in the adaptive weeks and months that follow, McWade offers valuable ideas that apply to the workplace, to relationships with children and in-laws, and to (ex) spouses.

ORDER FORM

NAME:_____

BILLING ADDRESS:_____

CITY:_____STATE:_____

COUNTRY:_____ZIP:_____

DAY PHONE:_____

E-MAIL:_____

PAYMENT METHOD:
    ☐ PAYMENT ENCLOSED, MAKE CHECKS PAYABLE TO CHAMPION PRESS LTD.

        ☐ VISA   ☐ MASTER CARD

NAME AS IT APPEARS ON CARD:_____

CARD NUMBER: _____

EXPIRATION DATE: _____

SIGNATURE: _____

Quanity	Name of Item	Total

                            Sub Total _____
              Sale Tax Wi residents 5.6%_____
S & H $4.00 1st item $1.00 each additional item _____
                                TOTAL _____

SEND ORDER TO: CHAMPION PRESS LTD
                       4308 BLUEBERRY ROAD
                       FREDONIA, WI **53021**